THE LIGHT THAT I CARRY IN ME

Marlon Medina

The Light That I Carry in Me. All rights reserved. Total or partial reproduction of this content is prohibited without authorization from the author, Marlon Medina.
Interior Layout and Cover Design: Mildres Sarai de la Cruz

English edition, June 2024

Dedication

The road has been long... and I am almost 40 years old, but I don't have those 40 years anymore! Those years are gone! And there is still so much to do.

I only have the present moment, and to reach this moment, I must thank all the teachers who have prepared the way before me. With effort, dedication, and total detachment, they have shared their light, their knowledge, and vision.

There is still much to learn and accomplish. but the load is lighter because God has surrounded me with a wonderful family.

Thanks to my friends from the past, who due to circumstances, are now distant. They were a blessing to me and are part of the treasures I carry in my heart.

Thank you to everyone who works tirelessly every day to create a brighter future for themselves and their loved ones.

Thank you, family. Thank you, friends. Thank you, brothers. Thank you, teachers. Thank you, fireproof women, thank you fire proof knights!

But above all, thank you, Father, because the inspiration is yours, and the honor is also yours. Thank you, thank you, thank you.

The Author.

The Light That I Carry in Me

INTRODUCTION

It was no longer me

The precise moment when you wake up, for a few seconds, and realize that you have become someone completely unknown, you recognize that your life is not how you want it to be, that your reality is completely different to what you once thought it could be.

It happened to me! For a moment I lost my way; a moment that lasted many years. Living with depression is not easy, and even more so pretending that everything was fine, pretending that I was conquering the world, when in reality it was the world and all I was carrying inside me, that was consuming me, that was destroying my life! Have you ever thought about what a person feels like, when they are about to die, drown in the sea?

I knew it, I was about to die that way, feeling that you start to swallow the salty water little by little, feeling that your body can't take it anymore, feeling the agony of knowing that you are seconds away from dying, trapped between the waves, the suffering and despair, but depression is much worse because in those moments in the water; the only thing I could think about was staying alive with all my strength! Unlike depression, in which I already felt dead, and the only thing I wanted was to disappear from the face of the earth, to no longer exist!

Fireproof Knights

The worst part of it all was that I didn't even know I had depression until much later. Without a doubt, it is a silent enemy! It traps you and slowly takes away your life, now that I think about it:
why?
When did I let it in?
How did it arrive?

It's just that it comes disguised; In my case, it came accompanied by news that would completely change my life, that would steal my excitement and the meaning of my reality. I remember: I was at work, when I was surprised by the presence of a family member, whom without empathy and in a dry and indifferent tone, told me: "Your brother has died! He was killed!" there were more words between the two of us, but my mind froze, on the same phrase "your brother has died!" Like an echo, unable to Speak Or react! My brother was everything to me, even though our relationship in recent years was not the best, we had beautiful memories of brotherhood. We suffered together, laughed and cried so many times, we experienced so many hardships and difficult situations, with the hope that one day we would live a better life and enjoy everything we desire as children. Even now, I miss him so much and I feel a lot of helplessness when I remember that moment. I believe there are moments that mark us, and that moment will stay with me forever, as one of the most difficult moments I have ever lived through.

During those moments I went through a very tough time, but I had to work to support my family, and with so many commitments and responsibilities on my shoulders, I had no other choice. I couldn't cry, I couldn't say goodbye to his body, or give him that final farewell. There were moments when I entered a state of denial, where I still expected a call from him, maybe it was all a lie, but I still held onto hope! This is something that many of us who live in a distant land go through, unable to return, seeking a better future for our loved ones; when my brother was no longer here, I lost the meaning of life, suddenly everything started to slowly turn gray. Something arose with his death, something grew inside me like weeds, and took hold of my thoughts and inhabited my heart; guilt and regret became present. Suddenly I began to remember all the bad things I did to my brother, how unfair, how cruel, the fights, the indifference, my hard heart when he needed me, believing that with that I was teaching him a lesson, when what I was really doing was wasting our last moments together here in this world. It's not a justification, but I didn't know what I was doing.

Now I understand the words of Master Jesus Christ, where he said, FORGIVE THEM, FATHER, BECAUSE THEY DON'T KNOW WHAT THEY DO.

Walking in the Valley of the Shadow of Death

There came a time when I realized that everything was a mess in my life. My thoughts were constantly blaming myself for everything. At my job, I was already working more than 16 hours a day. I think it was the only place where I felt useful, and at the same time, it was the only thing that helped me keep my mind busy. I waited and waited for something that would take away the pain that was eating me up inside, but I never told anyone. I didn't know how to express it, not even to those who talked about it. I put on the mask of a hard-working and responsible man. I often felt that I couldn't handle it anymore, but I still continued to *pretend that everything was fine.*

I was becoming a bad husband, a bad father, and a bad son. Alcohol had become a regular part of my routine, and I was constantly failing. Little by little, I became more focused on myself to the point where I completely forgot that my mother was also suffering, even more so than me. My wife was struggling and managing the household alone in my absence, and that my sister blamed herself, just like I blamed myself for the loss of our brother. Even my children went several days without seeing me; I was gone by the time they woke up, and I still hadn't returned from work when they went to sleep.

It was one of the many arguments I had with my wife, like usual, I ended up sleeping on the couch, when I couldn't hold back any longer, I sank to my knees and wept like a child. Between sobs I called out to God for help, I didn't want to live like this, but deep in my heart I knew that even in this darkness, there might be a ray of glimmer, a sign, something! Whatever! Before I fell asleep, my final thoughts were a desperate plea for help.

There is a biblical passage that provides guidance for when we are facing very difficult times: CALL TO ME AND I WILL ANSWER YOU.

The Light That I Carry in Me

Fireproof Knights
NOTES

The Light That I Carry in Me

CHAPTER 1

The number 7

What follows may seem unbelievable or exaggerated, but assistance arrived in the small form of the number 7.

When I woke up after that terrible night, upon opening my eyes and looked at my left arm (which had served me as a pillow), there was a small mark on it, a number 7. I tried to erase it with saliva, but it didn't come off. Instead, it looked like a small seal. The first thing I did was look up the meaning of the number 7 on the internet. To my surprise, the first thing I found said, **"have faith, help is coming."**

Later, I wanted to reread the message, but I couldn't find it! I only found a lot of information about the number 7, and its meaning, but not the message that I read before. I took it on faith, and I was fine.
I kept repeating to myself, "Help is coming."

I remained alert and hopeful, that something extraordinary would happen, but the day went by, without any such event. Suddenly, I felt the need to take a walk. I left work and just walked. While passing by a friends' business, I decided to stop by to say hello, because I was impressed by the appearance of the

Fireproof Knights

place on the outside. I said to myself, "I want to see, how my friends are doing"

Upon entering, I noticed a different glow in one of my friend's looks. I greeted her, and in her hug, I felt a different energy. When I saw her face, I noticed that she was very happy, and honestly, I was not paying attention to the conversation because my mind was concerned with what had happened to me that morning and the mark on my arm. My friend noticed the difference in my expression; she and I had contrasting energies. She asked me, "are you okay?"

And I told her that I was not feeling well. "I would like to have what you have", I said, "just for a moment, to feel as alive and full of life as you do! Just for a moment!" I considered confessing that I frequently had suicidal thoughts but I chose to remain silent!

She told me about a place, where she received a lot of help, to become the woman she is now. I thought, "I have to go! Is this the sign I was waiting for?"

I asked for information about the place, I said goodbye to my friend, and told her that I would go! In less than three weeks, I set out in search of that help. Because I had reached my limit, I couldn't take it anymore!

I was tired of being the person I was and doing the things I did, of living without purpose, and especially of feeling ashamed. I was so ashamed! I would look in the mirror, and hate the reflection staring back at me. I had to be okay, especially for my children!

I remember, when I was younger, I made a promise to myself

that: if God gave me the chance to be a father! I would be present for my children, I would provide them with, what I never had, but most importantly, I would give them the love of a father- a love I never experienced!

It is challenging to grow up without a father, even though my mother did everything she could to provide me with opportunities that she did not have; a father figure is still essential and so important in a man's life.

Please, if you are going through something very terrible, pause and ask for help! Your life is valuable, and I assure you that God is by your side even in this moment of darkness. Do not give up! Help is coming! **Have faith and take action!**

What if what you think it is, isn't what it seems?

Already on the road, I had all kinds of doubts. "What are you doing?" I just told myself, "Don't you see that you don't need help?". "You're fine, that's for weak people". Hundreds of excuses ran through my head, to go back and not face something unknown. I was scared because I didn't know what to expect!

Finally, I arrived at my destination and I surrendered myself to its hands. For the first time, I felt so uneasy, filled with doubts and fears. I found myself in the company of a jury, a judge, a large group of individuals who, like me, were guilty and an endless number of victims.

Fireproof Knights

As time went by, I found myself explaining my situation to numerous individuals, far more than I would have anticipated. I shared the reasons for my presence, feeling a deep sense of discomfort as I shared my pain, suffering, guilt, and justifications. Despite my overwhelming guilt, I was determined to endure and confront everything, as I had convinced myself that I deserved punishment. I believed it was the price I had to pay, even if it meant publicly humiliating myself.

It was a hard process. At times I realized that I was being manipulated, and I continued because I had no other way to heal. I trusted too much, but as I made progress something changed—everything had a purpose! Suddenly, the group of strangers to which I belonged, began to show sensitivity towards each other. We stopped being judgmental and started to feel deep empathy. We recognized that we are constantly navigating through life, wearing endless masks and playing the roles that correspond to us at all times. The world is like a theater, where drama, comedy, and action are all part of the show, influenced by beliefs and various tricks that hinder us from seeing the truth. But what is the truth? I asked myself this question, without receiving an answer.

During this rehearsal, as I took on the role of captain, I found myself leading a group of peers who were like brothers and sisters to me. It was the first time, for some of us, to progress from a starting point to an advanced level, where the seeds of leadership began to grow. After breaking barriers, we finally managed to reach our safe harbor.

In total, it was about three months from the first time I set foot in that place, until the last time I was there. After 3 months

The Light That I Carry in Me

of studying, embracing a new philosophy, and empowering myself, I now believed in my capabilities. I am a man with willpower, achievements and strength! This was my motto during the final stage of my journey, and it stirred a lot within me. I repeated it like a mantra every day, constantly.

When I ventured back into the world, I encountered a vastly different reality. Gradually, my old habits resurfaced, and the demons that had tormented me for so long reappeared! Almost as if they were mocking me. They told me, "Where, where is the man with willpower, achievements and strength?"

It was very difficult not to fall. I stood firm for as long as I could, but thoughts of suicide resurfaced, with voices urging me to end my life. It was a constant battle in my mind. One night, I couldn't bear the pain in my heart any longer, and it began to fail. I felt death looming once again as my health declined. I also experienced gallbladder attacks, and everything I ate caused me pain. I couldn't comprehend what was happening to me. It was frustrating to have acquired so much information during the three months of learning, yet not have the ability to improve my life! I felt as if I were truly traversing a desert. I realized that I just had to keep walking and searching for the path that would lead me to a better destination.

We only remember God when we need him! And indeed, I also fell into that error. When I found myself afflicted and once again dejected by the circumstances, I remembered Him again. And always, like a faithful and compassionate father, God sent me help again!

Fireproof Knights

An Encounter with My Creator

I prayed for several days, unsure how, but it was very clear in my mind that I was being heard. I requested an opportunity to rid myself of everything that was afflicting me.

It was one night, and I was not expecting a call that would change the course of my life forever. Mari Carmen, a longtime friend told me, when I answered the call, "I have something for you, and it is from God! But you have to come... Please don't ask any more questions, just come." It was almost 8 o'clock at night. After contemplating going for a few minutes, I said to myself "Marlon, once again you have asked for help through prayer, and God has sent you a friend and a gift. What are you waiting for? Just go!" I took a leap of faith and departed.

When I arrived at her house, she had arranged her patio for me with candles and white sheets. There were several beautiful trees that made me feel at peace. She had prepared such a beautiful and humble space, but you could see the love and appreciation in the air. The aroma of frankincense and myrrh made me feel safe and eager to know what this was all about!

She asked me to pray and give thanks to God that night. When I looked up at the sky, I realized that the moon was shining on us— a beautiful full moon. She told me that everything had a touch of magic and spirituality. She said: "For me it is a privilege to share this gift with you. I received precise instructions from God to give it to you."

I was speechless; I didn't know how to respond other than

The Light That I Carry in Me

saying thank you! With intrigue, I asked:

"Could you please explain what this is all about?"

She responded, "I tried to leave the explanation for last because I wanted to feel like I was making the right decision, and to see how you've coped with everything. You have confirmed to me that it is for you. What I am going to tell you is a secret. It is not for everyone. I am going to show you how to connect with the source, with the light, with God- and that my friend, is the gift I have for you."

We performed a series of simple but sacred steps, and afterwards she guided me to take deep breaths. Gradually, everything began to take on a different radiance. She asked me to recline on a sofa, that she had prepared for me with white sheets, and instructed me to get comfortable, and follow her guidance. As I breathed and followed her soothing voice, I entered into a deep meditation. Slowly, I concentrated on the present moment and felt my body relaxing more and more. Minutes passed, and suddenly, I sensed that my body was present but I felt as if I were outside of it, as if I were floating. Then, I experienced a beautiful and bright golden yellow light approaching the crown of my head.

From the moment it entered my mind and gradually descended until it reached my heart, I suddenly felt a presence so beautiful that I wish I had the ability of a poet to describe the wonderful sensation I experienced. So much love, peace, light, energy, and so much more...

I immediately recognized that I was in the presence of my

creator, and the first thing I felt was shame, I did not feel judged at any time, but I was overwhelmed by all the occasions where I had failed, and I could only begin to ask for forgiveness. It wasn't that God was asking me to do it; I just felt in my being that it was the right opportunity to do it. I found myself, from one moment to the next, asking for forgiveness for everything that came to mind, stored in my memory. With each word out of my mouth, I felt like a weight was lifted from my being. The more I asked for forgiveness, the lighter my body felt, until I felt like I was floating.

And I felt like I had become a little child, lulled to sleep by my creator. With a breath, I said, "thank you," and suddenly his presence left. A different but familiar presence came to me: my brother Alex. I felt his hug and immediately asked for his forgiveness. He stopped me with one word, "brother!" And he continued, "I have nothing to forgive you for. It was my decisions that led to my death. I didn't know what I was doing! But don't worry, I'm fine now. I'm at peace and happy." I told him that I missed him and that I loved him very much. I longed for one last hug. To feel at peace and experience a moment of indescribable happiness.

I opened my eyes to find my friend on her knees, praying for me. With tears in my eyes, I told her thank you, thank you, thank you, as many times as I could. I kissed her forehead, I hugged her, and explained her what I had experienced. She was happy and told me, "I knew you would make it!" I shared everything with her, and she listened patiently and with emotion. I couldn't contain my happiness. I felt at peace, forgiven, and free. I felt everything.

She asked me, "Do you know how much time has passed?" I

The Light That I Carry in Me

answered, "40 minutes, maybe an hour," and she told me: "It's been 5 hours or so." I paused and said, "How?" She responded, "Time in God's presence is relative! It behaves differently than what we are used to."

She told me, "It is time for you to return home. When the time is right, we will talk more about this. For now, rest and continue to give thanks! That will prepare you for greater opportunities and achievements."

From that day, nothing would be the same again!

You will never be the same after experiencing the presence of God. Now the question is, will I be ready for what is coming?

Fireproof Knights

The Light That I Carry in Me

Everything has a beginning

Everything has a beginning, and it is through a decision that a new reality begins to be contemplated!

For many days, I continued to replay in my mind everything I experienced that night. Memories of the past came flooding back, bringing with them a range of emotions. It felt as though I had stumbled upon a portal to connect with my inner self.

After a few days, I spoke with my friend, who has now become a spiritual guide for me. Always, as kind as she is, she told me, "I am your friend, and what you experienced is just the beginning of a very long and difficult path. That is why there are few who travel it. It goes as far as you feel the call, as the first step. I will tell you that you have to start by taking better care of yourself, and when you can see clearly, you will be able to help others understand!"

The journey started with Mary Carmen, but I encountered several other spiritual guides along the way, including Mary, Cesar, Vero, Mama Eva, Lidia, Lucy and Luz. To many teachers, to numerous traveling companions, people whom I greatly admire, and who are also in search of the truth, beings of light, angels, and a group of individuals committed to making this world a better place, thank you brothers and sisters.

Knowledge came to me from various sources. My deep

meditations became deeper and more sublime, helping me find a purpose for my existence and a guide to live in a correct and adequate way for my own well-being.

Today, I have decided to share this knowledge with you with the sole intention of providing a glimmer of light, knowledge, and tools that will help you improve your life. By taking care of yourself, you will be able to prosper and in turn, help others find their way. Little by little, we can sow new seeds in the world, to yield better fruits in the years to come. Moreover, we hope that our children and our children's children, can inherit a better world to live in. It's in our hands!

Few Are the Chosen

Many are called, but few are chosen!

All this time, I held onto the false idea that I had to be a chosen one, that I would hear a voice calling me, by my first and last name, instructing me to come and follow. We are all children of God, and the call is for everyone! There is no discrimination in my Father's Kingdom. So, if the voice does not come from an external source! Who makes the choice?
We do.
We Decide for Ourselves! If we are ready to move forward and follow the steps that lead us to truth, freedom, happiness, to the Kingdom of God!

It is we! Who have to follow in the footsteps of Master Jesus, but

The Light That I Carry in Me

how do we know if it is our time? It's simply something you feel! You just feel it! For me, time brought about difficulty and challenges. I was tired of the life I was leading, of constantly hurting myself. I was exhausted from feeling guilty, about everything, from being a bad father, bad son, bad brother, and bad friend- everything was just bad!

I grew weary of feeling unworthy of love, of being both the victim and the perpetrator, I became tired of not knowing my life's direction, of not comprehending life's meaning, of walking aimlessly, I became tired of praying for a better world, hoping for a Hollywood-like arrival of the master Jesus to end all the bad, I grew tired of waiting and chose to contribute to the solution, I became tired of merely identifying as a Christian and strived to embody Christ's teachings.

And it is at this moment that I ask you:
Are you already fed up? Or do you want more? Would you like to heal?
Do you want to stop doing evil?
Do you want to be part of the change?
Do you want to know the truth?
Do you want to live a paradise, here on earth?
Do you want to understand your purpose?
Do you want to be chosen?

If this is something you feel in your heart, then heed the call and take action! If you don't feel it yet, don't worry. You can continue reading because knowledge is for everyone! **The big difference lies in what we do with it!**

I invite you to improve and be happy!
What follows after this page will be at your discretion. I am not

Fireproof Knights

trying to change the way you act, think, or be. I wish the best for you, so if my words help you improve your life, heal, make you discern the reasons behind things, open your eyes to a reality different from the one you know, question everything and everyone, love yourself like never before, and truly know God! Then I will have accomplished my goal!

Don't just take my word for it. I encourage you to verify everything for yourself. See if it resonates with you, if it aligns with your inner self, and if you believe that, what I'm sharing with you has a positive impact on your life. Keep going and don't stop. Repeat and repeat any chapter that resonates with you.
Read this book in whatever order feels right to you, and above all, seek help if you need it!

This book is a conversation between friends! God bless you and thank you for your time, which is the most valuable thing we have!
I invite you to be the light this world needs!
Are you interested?

Let's get started!

The Light That I Carry in Me
CHAPTER 2

Truth is a Sphere

There is just one small detail: this is my truth, I invite you to see life through my eyes, gaining knowledge accumulated over many years, and most importantly, with the permission and inspiration of Father God!

Through my multiple meditations, I have received a wonderful gift, that has helped me understand a lot about life, and the reason behind so much. I still have much more to learn, but every day, I am dedicated to expanding my knowledge, so I can gain a deeper understanding, and at the same time, I respect and I understand, that we all know a truth! Each of us will have a unique interpretation of what our truth is. Because each person perceives the truth, from a unique perspective, shaped by their individual life experiences, the truth can be likened to a sphere. Its appearance varies depending on one's vantage point, leading to diverse interpretations of reality.

But how can we use this to our advantage? Let's acknowledge that we all desire a better life, filled with love, abundance, prosperity, happiness, peace, and every emotion that elevates a higher frequency.

So, what we must do is to look at the results, as my teacher Jesus said, "by their fruits you will know them." If the results you are obtaining, does not make you happy, then look for someone who is achieving results that you like, and make a conscious change. Emulate what this person does, imitate their habits, so that you can also achieve similar results. You cannot expect to get oranges if you are a bush of thorns, by the same principle, if you want to achieve more, acquire more, contribute more, and gain more from life, you must first plant a seed in fertile soil that will yield the fruits that you desire.

The mind is like soil! First, you have to recognize if it is: full of weeds or arid or dry and lifeless, or to a certain extent hostile. And begin to work on it, removing anything in the way and adding what it is needed. In a few months, the outcomes will change and your truth will have evolved. As a result, you will provide a different testimony, when this occurs, you will be prepared to make further adjustments at a more profound level, leading to better outcomes and so forth.

We will work to systematically uncover the obstacles holding us back, and identify the changes needed to elevate our lives, and reach the next level.

I guarantee that after we work together, you will undergo a transformation, realizing your true worth, to God and to yourself. And you will find yourself wanting more and more, in a healthy way, to enhance and improve in order to be more helpful, not for obligation, but more because you are born with the power to make a difference and help.

"A blessing is only truly a blessing, when it is shared"

The Light That I Carry in Me

Share the knowledge you have learned, even if it is with just one person, because when you teach, you learn again! Make a bet with a friend or loved one to see who can apply more of the knowledge contained in this book.

I believe it will be beneficial for all, because before writing it, I personally put what I say into practice and shared it with many of my friends and loved ones. "Yes, it works" and "Yes, you can have the life you've always wanted." Someone who is reaping abundant fruits for the glory of God, more than I ever thought possible, but still very little compared to what a child of God can get, and deserves, from this life is telling you, it's possible!

In case no one has told you today, "I LOVE YOU," I have been there too, I understand you and let me tell you that: You are not alone! Together we will go very far, because we are all children of the same Father. We may not always know what we are doing, but from now on, you will have the tools and knowledge to become a blessing to this world and to all the people who are part of it.

Fireproof Knights

Ferrari

A few years ago, I recall that one of my initial jobs in the United States was at a natural medicine store. The owner interviewed me for a sales position, and discussed the commission structure, emphasizing the potential for high earnings! However, she also stressed the importance of putting in a lot of effort, and maintaining a professional appearance, as in sales, perception often influences how you are treated. she instructed me to show up the next day at 9 a.m. to start working.

I remember that, I didn't have much money at the time, but I invested what I had in dress shirts, a pair of pants, and shoes to look good for my first week. With all the motivation in the world, I showed up to work feeling very nervous about everything I had to learn, at the same time, I felt excited because when I was a child, I always dreamed of being a doctor. I was thrilled by the idea of learning from a doctor. As she was a naturopath, for me that was the closest I had been to medicine.

I was waiting for my first class on natural medicine, to understand its importance and perhaps, gain a manual to learn how to help many people. I think it's something I always imagined doing. I had a whole rehearsed movie in my mind of what my first day at work would be like.

My reality was different. I remember she said to Carlos, one of her salespeople, "Show him, what is going to be his work about!"

The Light That I Carry in Me

So, Carlos handed me a stack of flyers and said, "Your task is to be out on the street, welcoming people. The goal is to persuade them to come in and buy medicines from us."

It definitely wasn't what I expected, in my mind had a lot of thoughts telling me to leave it, that, that job was not worth it, but at the end I decide to give thanks for the opportunity and I stopped complaining, and with a different attitude I began doing my job. As the weeks passed, I became accustomed to life on the street, facing rejection, and humiliation from various individuals, but the hot weather was the hardest in summer time! However, as someone who has always enjoyed challenges, my goal was to interact with as many people as possible, and get to the point when I also could be able to sale and earn more but overall, my focus was to maintaining a positive attitude in any circumstance!

Until one day, a gentleman approached me and said: "I'm going to ask you a question",
"Would you give a Ferrari to a person who doesn't know how to drive?"

I kept thinking as he said goodbye, and left without giving me an answer!
Since that day, I have carried that memory with me. Now, after several years, I finally understand the meaning of that question.

I AM THE FERRARI!

Unfortunately, we waste talents, youth, and life in the hands of *people who do not know how to guide us. And, how can we blame them? They went through the same situation. From now on, I understand that it is my responsibility to manage myself and bring out the best in me, I now realize that I am a child of God and, as such, I have the capacity to excel in the game of life, representing my Father's team. I aim to teach others that they have the potential to be like a Ferrari, not settling for less, being grateful for who they are at the present moment, but striving to become everything they can be.*

What has served me the most, is recognizing that: I do not always have control of my life. Many times, I do not know what I am doing, but I have faith that everything will always be fine! Because God is now by my side at all times. If I lose my way, I trust that he will be there to show me the right path.

The Ferraris also employ a team of individuals to help them improve their performance. It is okay to seek support from others when needed, to seek the right help and to be the right help. It is also important to be humble and recognize when we are not the best option. If I can contribute something to your life, count on me. If I'm not the right person, keep searching until you find the help you need. Don't give up, persist!

From one Ferrari to another, **"SUCCESS."**

The Light That I Carry in Me

CHAPTER 3

Take Responsibility of Yourself

The step to achieving complete freedom, and obtaining everything we desire in life! Is by taking responsibility for ourselves. For a long time, we blame everyone who crosses our path for our lives. As they say, we pin the blame on anyone but us.

As children, we begin our journey with our parents, who have the responsibility to support and guide us. In his absence, it is our grandparents' responsibility to ensure that we have everything. Next on the list are our favorite uncles. We seek out every available family member to "assist us", that is, to take responsibility for us.

But this is also something that we ask of teachers, friends, brothers, neighbors, acquaintances, and anyone who has even the slightest connection. They are all potential candidates.

Later, when we have a partner, we seek refuge in this special person to take care of our happiness. Since childhood, women have been told that Prince Charming would come to rescue them and provide them with their castle and everything they deserve. So, some! Buy the history and wait, and wait and wait. In my case, I used to think of myself as a Prince, and I would eagerly help damsels in "distress" whenever the opportunity arose.

Fireproof Knights

I forgot about myself and focused solely on providing and giving everything that, in my opinion, was expected of me, without even questioning, whether such sacrifices were necessary. I took on one burden without considering if there was a limit that needed to be respected.

Later, as years passed, the responsibility falls on our children to take care of us as we age. We believe that since we gave them life and took care of them, it is now their duty to look after us until the end.

I also need to mention the government, as it is often used as a primary excuse for not taking responsibility for our lives. We say, "because of the government," "because of the president," because of my boss-he pays us too little," "he doesn't pay us enough."

We often blame God for the suffering and challenges we face, hoping that through prayer and miracles our lives will improve and become perfect.

At the end, we await a savior who will come and put an end to all the evil in the world at once and take us to a paradise, where we can finally experience eternal happiness!

I won't deny that paradise exists, but we can begin experiencing it right here on earth.

The first step to living in such a beautiful way, regardless of our location, where abundance is present, and where we can have everything, we desire and more, is by "taking responsibility for ourselves."

The Light That I Carry in Me

If we do, we will cease being in a state of rest, in which we have remained for many years, and we will "activate."

When we release the notion that someone will come to rescue us, we become our own savior, and we start to perceive opportunities where previously we only saw obstacles. We will begin to flow in such a way that it seems like magic. Through effort, dedication, and hard work, we will begin to see better results. Money will suddenly begin to abound in our life, our work will improve, and everyone will want to be part of our life. They will no longer hide, thinking that we only come around when we have a problem to solve.

Problems will be for us now, blessings in disguise. We will do better. Suddenly, we will get better grades because now it is completely up to us. No one will help us with us assignments anymore. And that will begin to be a part of our life. We should take pride in everything we do, and it should be our mission to achieve better results in everything.

The most beautiful thing is that, by relying solely on ourselves, we are in complete control of our life. No longer have to tolerate any abuse out of necessity, lack of money, or because we don't know what to do with our life. No one will take advantage of us because we will not allow them to. If we find ourselves in a situation where we feel, we have no other option, it will be temporary! We will make it our mission to regain control of our life. We now will be able to bless and help others because we will have more than enough, and we will do it out of love, not because someone is playing the victim and seeking resolution in their life.

With our partner, the fairy tale will conclude, where no one will be a burden to anyone, but a blessing. You know the meaning of husband/wife? "Ideal help," and that is what both will become, constantly striving to help each other. Time can make our life very beautiful and blessed.

When we focus on ourselves and on all the talents that God has given us, we will realize that we have never really needed God in the way we thought. Instead of asking for miracles, we will become a miracle. We will seek God for advice, for friendship, and for love. Our relationship with God will be beautiful, and you will feel the warmth of a father, just as I do. You will not be alone anymore. Apart from God, do not forget that we have many brothers here on earth who are going through the same challenges and seeking a better place for everyone—a paradise here on earth.

Raise your awareness, take responsibility for your life, and lead by example. Take back control of yourself and do whatever makes you happy, in alignment with your true essence.

Blessings Always, Prosperity, Peace, Abundance, and Love every day of my life. By my decision, I take responsibility for my being, body, and life. I will use the talents that were given to me by my Heavenly Father at birth. It is my responsibility to discover and put them to use. As I do, I will be in better conditions to receive more and better talents, produce better results, and help and bless my life and that of all the people who are part of it. This is my decision, made without ties or obligations, always for love and for the love of my father, it is done, it is done, it is done in the name of I Am That, I Am.

The Light That I Carry in Me

Take Action

After realizing that we are the only ones responsible for being able to change our lives, we ask ourselves, "What's next?"

Now, my friend, begins the battle of a war that will likely last our entire lives—a war whose battlefield is our mind. The enemy is within us, "the sin that dwells in me," occupying a place that does not belong to it and controlling us without our awareness, manipulating us, and making us slaves to its will. That is why this will require everything we have, and are, to tilt victory in our favor. It is not for everyone. But if you are already weary of carrying everything, if you are tired of feeling unhappy and relying on others for your happiness, if you feel that life no longer holds meaning, if you believe your life has a purpose but you have lost your way, if you crave justice and believe you deserve a better life, if you feel you have not yet given your best.

If you feel like you've let everyone down, including yourself and God, and you're ashamed of it, if you want to do things right, but don't know how, if you don't understand the meaning of life and want to find out, if you no longer want to live in fear, if you're ready to confront your demons and take control of your life. If you are ready to heal, love, be happy, and live a full life filled with experiences that make you sigh with emotion.

So, we need a compelling reason to pursue the life we desire. Without a strong "why," it will be challenging to achieve our goals. It is very clear and defined why we should continue fighting. If we are defeated in the first battles, we must find a reason within ourselves that overcomes all fear, obstacles, and doubt.

Fireproof Knights

In me, I carry five very clear reasons why I have to win the war against the evil within me.

First of all, there is God. I was not always like this. I used to think about everything, but I never included Him in my life. Now it is different. For me, He is everything, and it is out of love for Him that I have decided to give the best of myself and to make the most of all the talents God has given me. I am grateful for the life God has given me, for saving me from death, for freeing me, for healing my body, soul, and being, and for giving me the opportunity to be a dad.

I am one of the most important reasons because I have discovered that I cannot give, if I do not have. How can I help others? If I am not in a position to do so? Yes, I am the one who needs help. How can I help without selflove?
To love without having love in my heart is like having dirt in my own eye and focusing on the mote of my brother's eye, I have to clean my eye first to see clear and then help my brother take away the mote.

My children are one of the most important reasons for me to strive for the life I deserve. From the moment I found out I would be a father, a strong desire to provide them with the best in life was born within me. However, in prioritizing their needs for so long, I ended up sacrificing too much of myself. My stress, anger, and frustration were often directed at them. I realized that I had been striving to give them things they didn't even ask for, mistakenly believing that this made me a good father. I now understand that true happiness and love are what truly matter,

The Light That I Carry in Me

and I am committed to filling their lives with both.

My family, my mother, for giving me life, my wife, for her unconditional love, and my brothers, for their support—motivates me to fight and make an effort, to have the possibility of giving them what they deserve and to always support them. They are a fundamental pillar in my life, and above all, a very important reason not to give up.

My aspiration is to always strive for more, because only by having more can I reach more places and have the possibility of collaborating to provide others with the opportunity to live a dignified life. With more, I can offer the chance for education, access to clean water, and even a Christmas gift. Having more enables me to support foundations that bring rays of hope to entire communities around the world. By having more, we can consider others and give back some of the blessings we receive every day, thanks to our heavenly father.
It is sad! That many children around the world suffer from food insecurity, while some people amass wealth to validate, their worth and existence.

I believe that everything will change for the better. I am confident that by awakening our awareness, we can make a difference in the world.

That is why I thank you for fighting the most important battle of your life—the battle for yourself. Find as many reasons as you can and write them down. Keep them close to you, and read them daily. Make it one of the first things you look at when you get up, especially on those days when you don't want to do it, on those days when you want to throw in the towel and give up.

Fireproof Knights

Defeated. Remember your reasons for persevering. If you need to rest, allow yourself a brief moment, because the inner force that opposes us never rests; it is always waiting for an opportunity to exploit our carelessness and make us stumble.

Stay alert at all times. As we progress through the pages, we will discover tools to shift the battle in our favor and regain control of our lives. Have faith and don't give up. It's for them, for the people who depend on us, and it's for us. This applies to everyone.

Let's Go!

The Light That I Carry in Me

CHAPTER 4

⚜

About us?

We need to truly understand who we are, taking the time to explore every detail of who we are, including the aspects we perceive as negative, positive or neutral. Gather as much information as possible and begin documenting everything in a notebook. The goal is not to deceive or appear favorable, but to remain impartial. The aim is to gather as much information as possible to gain a better understanding of our current situation and to focus on making improvements.

Without a clear understanding of what we are going to work on, it would take us more time to correct, improve, and heal. Without knowing our preferences, thoughts, desires, capabilities, fears, and the things or people we dislike, we love, or are indifferent to.

All this information necessary for improvement and to discover the reason behind our decisions? Why do we tend to favor a posture of observation? Why do certain types of people attract our attention more than others? Why do we prefer certain perfumes over others? Why do we reject a flavor or an aroma? Why?

All these "why?" "It is not important to have all the answers, only to get to know why we strive for, will be beneficial. The goal is to understand ourselves better and to truly comprehend our desires."

So many times, I made decisions without understanding why? So many times, I chose a person without knowing why. So many times, I failed without understanding why? So many things I did wrong without a specific answer as to why? That made me understand a convincing reason for the intense feelings of hatred. Sadness, or emotion that arose in the presence of someone or something without being invited. Why do I react this way? Why do I behave like this?

Write down your discoveries, and as you continue, you will find that doing so clarifies your thoughts and gradually helps your mind to comprehend. If you haven't found the answers yet, don't worry; everything will come in due time. Sometimes we are not prepared to know. Trust the process and respect everyone's journey.

We often believe that other people are fundamentally different from us, when in reality we share many common experiences. Regardless of our backgrounds, all of us encounter unwanted situations, we all have fears to conquer, and face doubts, curiosities, and challenges. To win, we all need to have a better understanding of ourselves and what we want from life. Often, we seek understanding from others, when in reality, we struggle to understand us, so many times, we cannot even understand ourselves.

Let's take the time to discover how wonderful we can be. Let's explore the capabilities of our bodies—running faster, jumping higher, and excelling in sports. Let's also uncover the potential of our minds and all that we can achieve.

The Light That I Carry in Me

We are capable of learning and creating. Let's discover new skills, explore our potential, and put it to the test day by day. Let´s approach life with the curiosity of children, eager to know, learn, and live!

Fireproof Knights

NOTES

The Light That I Carry in Me

CHAPTER 5

⚜

With Our Thoughts, We Change Our World!

It all starts in our minds; it's as simple as that. Something that I am very clear about is that our reality is shaped by our thoughts. We must modify the programming within ourselves in order to change our external reality.

From a very young age, thoughts, traditions, idioms, ideologies, ways of being, thinking, and acting are instilled in us through our environment. Whether through our parents, friends, teachers, siblings. The government or society itself. Our upbringing is influenced by the location of our birth. And that's ok, because at that time a better way to educate, teach, and transmit correct knowledge to the beings who began in this world was unknown. In the past, knowledge was not readily accessible to everyone; it was reserved for a select few. Even today, despite the abundance of tools for learning, self-improvement, and life transformation, many individuals have been conditioned to think in a certain way for so long that adopting a different mindset seems illogical.

Repetition is the process through which a new thought or habit becomes integrated into our programming. You might feel like I´m comparing us to computers, but in truth, our brains function in a similar way. We possess the most powerful computer that

Fireproof Knights

exists, but we have constrained its limits.

Let's start by putting a distinct program in our mind, when we are watching television, you are influencing your thoughts and behaviors. How many times have you seen action scenes with actors driving at high speeds, only to feel the urge to do the same? Or witnessed a character successfully wooing someone, and then attempted to replicate it? Perhaps after a horror movie, you found yourself feeling uneasy and even afraid to turn off the lights! Television has the power to program your mind in unexpected ways. And there are many examples like these. You just have to wake up and see that in reality, we have given up our creative power to external factors.

What if we start to take back control of our lives and reprogram our minds with thoughts, that align more with our desires and passions? How about we start creating paradise here on earth!

Let's begin by avoiding things that we know can hurt us or bring negative energy into our lives, such as listening to sad music, watching violent movies, or consuming unpleasant news. With just that change, in a few days, we will feel an increase in our energy and notice that everything has a different shine.

I know it can be difficult to control our thoughts. It is always challenging, for me as well, but it is possible, and that is all we need — for it to be possible! This gives us hope, that it can be accomplished. And always remember, if someone else has already done it, then it is possible for you.

Don't underestimate the power of taking baby steps; it's **consistency** that will work miracles. The more you tip the

The Light That I Carry in Me

balance toward a type of thinking that aligns with the reality that interests you, the closer you get to making what you want a reality. Remember: "If you can see it in your mind, you can hold it in your hand"

Create the vision that you want for your life and have it written as clear as possible, so anyone can understand it and get inspire by it, and keep it in your mind and heart and all will move to give opportunity for its materialization.

Fireproof Knights
NOTES

The Light That I Carry in Me

CHAPTER 6

❧

Don't Use God's Name in Vain

More than just a commandment, it is a rule for our own benefit. Do you know the name of God?

God, with His immense intelligence, was so wise that by naming himself, He included Himself with us! Embracing unity with us. His name is "I AM."
Now, how many times do we use his name in vain? Let me tell you something: the word has a creative power and we often create things that we do not want, because of our own mouth, we said things like:
I am poor.
I am stupid.
I am slow.
I am a bad father.
I am a bad son.
I am a bad husband.
I am a bad mother.
I am a bad woman.
I am bad man.
I am ugly.
I am unlucky.

You, see? We often use God's name in vain, and aside from

feeling remorseful, we inadvertently attract unwanted things into our lives. Consequently, we may wonder why things are not going well for us. We are in control of our destiny, but just as it took time for us to find ourselves in the hole where we often feel stuck, it will also take time to break free and transform our lives, leading us to a new place. A different plane. Be patient, but **consistently take action**. *Remember the importance of "repetition."*

If you find yourself thinking negative thoughts or using God's name in vain, now you know that it is not right because it is not good for you. Do not even think that God punishes you. The punishing God does not exist. We ourselves have created a novel.

Remember to use God's name in a respectful and positive manner, empowering yourself and fostering a sense of vitality.
I AM STRONG
I AM GRATEFUL
I AM INTELLIGENT
I AM WORTHY OF RECEIVING LOVE
I'M HAPPY
I AM ABUNDANT
I AM PROSPEROUS
I AM BLESSED
I AM THE SON OF GOD
I'M A GOOD SON
I AM A GOOD HUSBAND
I AM A GOOD FATHER
I AM AN EXCELLENT HUMAN BEING
I AM A BLESSING TO ALL
I AM A BEING OF LIGHT
I AM LOVE
I AM LIGHT

The Light That I Carry in Me

And it is not about telling lies, it is about speaking into existence that what we want to become!

I also ask you to keep present that "I AM" is the name of GOD. Many do not know it, and use it for their EGO, but coming from the ego has a different feeling. When you use it, you feed more into the EGO. Many times, you succeed in life because you have found your passion, put in effort, and managed to get ahead. Now, you may think it is solely thanks to your own efforts, forgetting that many people have helped you reach where you are, and that GOD has given you the talent to achieve your current position. However, you may then say:

I am the best; no one can beat me. I am very cool.
I am powerful and invincible.
I am so skilled that I can start from scratch and do it all over again, anew.
I am the best.

We can be one with God and be more, or we can be one without God, and use his name in vain and feel constantly alone, and have also the feeling that life is so hard and challenging, and that nobody understands! When in reality we are the ones that do not understand life!

The problem is that we are NOT approaching life with humility and in accordance with the law. Someone who is haughty and arrogant creates an atmosphere of rejection wherever they go. They seek out people for recognition to feel flatter and praised, but they are so blind to the fact that they are causing a division among others. Many people even go so far as to say, "I hope things go badly for him, so that his presumption goes away." Be careful, as this energy can move away from abundance and make it feel like we are asking life to take everything from us, just to *prove that we are "so good, that we can do everything again very easily" Let's not complicate our life! If we find ourselves in that mindset, we just need to acknowledge our mistake and adjust our attitude. It's not that we're successful just because our own effort, there is something more; We can surely have many talents, have worked so hard, and developed many habits over time. We may deserve a lot from life, and God blesses us. However, it's important to do things the right way so that God can bless us even more, and let's not' risk what we have just to learn a lesson! We have to "acknowledge" the sources of our inspiration, health, and intelligence, and to express gratitude for these, as well as for the people who have supported us along the path to our current success. If we are there, I guarantee that one way or another, Someone! Has helped us at some point. When employers speak to their employees in a disrespectful manner, insult them, and exploit their need for work to humiliate them, "it's not acceptable." Because if it weren't for employees there were not a business!*

Honor God every time you use his name, and consider what comes after I Am! Be prudent and respectful, and you will see how your life transforms for the better, when you apply this principle.

Sometimes we ask without even aware that we are asking for, and we invite lessons to happen, experiences to happen, all because we don't take the time to really think through what we are speaking!

Ask in a Good Way

The Light That I Carry in Me

The apostle James already said, "You ask, but you ask wrong." If I am doing it wrong, how can I do it right?

We need to be cautious when making requests, because we are often unsure of what we truly desire. We may believe we want something, only to realize later that we don't. Rushing through life can lead to unnecessary complications, so it's best to pause. And consider whether what we are about to request is actually what we desire.

What is the purpose of our ask? It is important to recognize the profound connection between our heart and the words that come out of our tongue. Superficial questioning may lead to obtaining things that do not contribute to our lives. Or we will request things for which we are not prepared. For example, when we ask for strength, it is highly likely that we will face tests that will make us stronger. Do we really want that? Or, we prefer to be more specific and ask for a talent or virtue to better handle a particular situation.

We seek wisdom, and in my case in particular, I have encountered various problems, difficulties, illnesses, and obstacles that, I now bless because they have transformed me into someone very prepared to face difficulties and challenges on my path. But if I had known all that was coming to me, I would have asked in a better way. You can also acquire wisdom through study, conversations, reading, observation, seeking advice from the right people. It is important to pay attention to the accomplishments of others and the efforts they make to achieve them. This allows me to decide whether to emulate their actions or pursue my own path based on my desires and what I deserve.

Sometimes, when we ask for a job, we are asked what kind of

Fireproof Knights

job we are seeking. Desperately, we respond with "whatever." At first, we put our best intentions into learning and doing our best on the job. However, sooner or later, we realize that either we don't like it or it wasn't the right thing for us to do. That we expected, or requires a high level of responsibility, discipline, or qualities that we do not possess, and we are simply not interested in acquiring. Therefore, the best thing we can think of is to start complaining about the job, the boss, or the colleagues. Instead of dwelling on the wrong decision, let's be grateful for the opportunity, keep our options open, and seek something that aligns more with our goals and interests.

Sometimes we seek the love of a specific person, only to realize that being with that person doesn't meet our expectations. This may not be because the person is bad, but rather because we often focus on superficial aspects such as appearance or material possessions. In reality, the most crucial element in a relationship is the mutual feeling experienced when together—the chemistry, the sense that nothing else matters, the opportunity to share moments, and the feeling that time stands still, creating a little piece of paradise here on earth.

At the university, there are many people who, from a young age, have been inspired by characters in novels or movies, such as doctors, lawyers, or engineers. It's common for us to declare, "I'm going to be a doctor when I grow up," for example, and then confidently share this career aspiration with others, hoping that our childhood dreams will come true. When the time comes, we go to university to study what we've always wanted. However, we often realize too late that it's definitely not for us.

If, on the contrary, we took the time to think and feel whether

The Light That I Carry in Me

what we are about to invite into our lives is truly what we desire, things would be very different. Many people would be pursuing their passions and developing the talents they were born with, on this earth.

That is why it is always necessary to know what do you want from life? What experiences do you want to have?
And why?

And this go hand I hand, when using the name of God because we will speak into existence only what it is in accordance with the kind of life we want, with the kind of experiences we would like to have, we just need to be aware of the way we speak, and don't worry if there are times when we do it wrong, the important thing here is to acknowledge when we are not speaking well and correct ourselves and keep on trying until it becomes natural.

Fireproof Knights
NOTES

The Light That I Carry in Me

CHAPTER 7

⚜

Everything has a frequency

When we realize that everything that exists has a unique frequency, it's like a label, a distinctive and exclusive identification to recognize its designated place. With this understanding, we will realize that everything is where it should be, ranging from very low frequencies such as shame, guilt, apathy, suffering, fear, desire, anger, and pride. Then they begin to rise until they reach the maximum frequency: courage, neutrality, will, acceptance, reasoning, love, joy, peace, and enlightenment.

The lower our frequency, the closer we are to illness, and even death or suicide. That's why it's important to help people who are experiencing these feelings, because at that point, all similar thoughts vibrate. Therefore, it's not surprising that someone on a frequency like that experiences a turn of bad luck. In these low frequencies, we encounter poverty, lack, diseases, plagues, lies, sadness, heartbreak, hopelessness, attachment, low passions, depression, suicides, homicides, and all types of violence—emotional, mental, and physical. Reasoning is severely limited, and it can lead to extreme and deplorable situations where people wish to cease to exist, seeing death as a gift.

Many people have reported experiencing a state like this, where

Fireproof Knights

they heard voices that mocked and incited them to end their lives, voices that tormented them constantly. I know I did! It is not easy to be going through this. It is for this reason that we must always be compassionate with everyone because, in reality, we do not know what battles they are fighting internally.

On the other hand, all the emotions that range from will to enlightenment, the latter being the highest frequency that we have managed to comprehend, carry with them various positive outcomes of equal frequency, such as: health, prosperity, abundance, order, beauty, understanding, humility, brotherhood, goodwill, appreciation of everyone and everything, love of nature, appreciation of beauty, recognition, intelligence, wisdom, detachment, equality, tranquility, and inspiration to create various improvements in life. That is why when you are in love, it is easy to believe, to create, to imagine, to dream, and to think. Everything flows effortlessly, like a spring of water. Living is a blessing, and life takes on an impressive brilliance and beauty. Everything becomes easier, everything syncs up, and all kinds of magical moments happen. In those frequencies, the impossible becomes possible, and miracles happen.

As within, so without. When experimenting intense emotions, the frequency will attract similar things in the world around you. As a result, things will change, and it is at that moment when you have to learn to let go and embrace discomfort, because new experiences often bring new people, things and opportunities such as a new job or new experiences. It's a time for all things to be made new, a new heaven and a new earth!

Many times, you may feel like you don't fit in or belong to a place. You might feel alone, misunderstood, or even feel like others are against you in some way. The opposite will happen

The Light That I Carry in Me

when you get to where you should be. Everything will fall into place, and you will feel like people speak your language. You will feel that everything is flowing, and you will feel happy, loved, and appreciated. Now, everything you ever dreamed of is within your reach.

You have to let go. There are people who will cling to you and prevent your growth. Even you will have moments of doubt, fear, and anxiety. It is in those moments that you have to trust the process, believe! And have faith in God and in yourself. This is a price that must be paid, and the people who truly love you and want the best for you, will understand it. Better yet, they will want to follow your example, and accompany you on the journey. They will also seek a way to reach that new heaven and new earth.

Everything has a frequency but many things share frequencies that are alike, so it is said: "if you want to have something out of life match the frequency of that with you", so there is an alignment and the vibration resonates one with the other. So, it is also said that: "what you look is also looking for you"

Fireproof Knights
NOTES

The Light That I Carry in Me

CHAPTER 8

❦

Express What You Feel

Often, we are unsure of what we want, but our feelings can guide us and help us determine if we are on the right path or not.

What it is important, is to be aware of our emotions at all times and communicate them appropriately. Perhaps it's a bit challenging for us because, since we were children, we were not allowed to do it. Maybe we had to be quiet, or perhaps someone told us, not to get involved in conversations. In my case, I didn't have anyone to talk to, because my mother worked all the time, to provide for me and my siblings, and I didn't have a father who was around. I didn't have the right people to learn from. I learned my lessons from movies, cartoons, friends who were in similar situation as me, strangers, or simply imitating the way others expressed their feelings. I wasn't sure if it was the correct way, but it was the only way I knew!

Now, I understand that the correct way, is through open conversation. We need to learn to communicate without passing judgment, making complaints, or expressing preferences. We should refrain from playing the victim or trying to influence decisions. Simply daring to be vulnerable and open our hearts is beneficial when we have someone to express ourselves to, but we can also have a solitary conversation with God. He will always be there for us. Pay attention and listen to your body. When we react *to something, it indicates that we are on the right track. Our body is wise and will communicate discomfort through tears, facial expressions, involuntary movements, heavy breathing, or breathing problems. Just pay attention. Please identify the location of the damage that caused it.*

If, on the contrary, you want to know if you are on the right path or doing the right thing, close your eyes and pay attention to your feelings. Identify how that situation or person makes you feel. Do you feel peace and love? Are you seeking happiness, strength, confidence, and enthusiasm? How, are you feeling? To be honest, many times, we are unsure of our true desires and we deceive ourselves, and others by claiming to feel emotions, that we do not truly experience. We may say "I love you" out of obligation, in response to the other person's declaration, even when we do not genuinely feel it. Being alone can be confusing, leading us to mistake it for love or to seek something in return, rather than risk the pain of expressing our true feelings. Honesty is essential for us. We may deceive everyone, but eventually, we will face severe consequences for not being honest from the start. Don't complicate your life alone; it's not worth it.

By not being honest about our feelings, we prolong situations, sometimes for years. It would have been better, to tell the truth in time. Some people are only passing through our lives; they fulfill their purpose and that's it.

What emotions do you experience when you are in a determining place? Do you feel apathy, acceptance, peace, or love? Do you experience a positive or negative vibe? Many times, we tolerate people's shortcomings and give them underserved opportunities, thinking we are being kind. In reality, we may be shielding them from facing the truth until they reach a crisis

The Light That I Carry in Me

point. This is often the case. But since we want to avoid that, we allow them to take advantage of our goodwill. When someone needs help, they ask for it! If they don't need it, don't give it! Let them express also what they feel and what they need, I understand that sometimes it is so hard because the person going thru a hardship, is someone we care deeply; but there are lessons we all need to face, to help us elevate our awareness.

Fireproof Knights
NOTES

The Light That I Carry in Me

CHAPTER 9

⚜

The True Teachers

Taking into perspective that life is a school, we will look at everything and everyone as opportunities for growth and learning. Difficult situations, such as illnesses, broken hearts, breakups, and failures, reveal who we can trust, teach us patience, and demonstrate what truly matters in life. They also prompt us to appreciate what we have and show us the path to resilience. These experiences help us cultivate humility and gain a new perspective on life. They actually demonstrate our unity, bring out the best is us, and also reveal our worst.

They help us understand where our faith lies, marking a distinct before and after. We will never be the same after crossing the desert, but these experiences are necessary as they are a part of life. "What is not necessary is more suffering".

We are all students, and we are all teachers. There is always something new to learn, and you will always encounter someone who doesn't know what you know.

In ancient times, tribes would gather around a campfire to share stories and knowledge, passing them down from generation to generation. Jesus frequently spoke with his disciples, but it was during the Holy Supper that he urged them to commemorate him by doing what he did. For me, he was not only talking about

Fireproof Knights

bread and wine but rather about sharing the word of life, because man does not live by bread alone!

When we sit for dinner with our family and discuss the day's events, we often reenact the same scene without investing the necessary intention into it. Learn and teach! Because those are the moments that remain most vivid in our minds and hearts. These are unique moments, especially for the little ones. They hold deep and beautiful meanings, but we often fail to make the most of them. Instead of discussing what is truly important and can improve our lives, we talk about everything else and neglect the underlying reasons for things. We are often hesitant to share our feelings, advice, or life plans, and instead, we allow television, cell phones, and other forms of technology to educate us. We should seize this crucial and meaningful time to impart what truly is important in life.

Time is one of the greatest teachers. Through it, we will find a satisfying solution to various difficulties. The only thing we can truly count on is the time we have. It is important to constantly remember this, and decide how to invest it, in a way that enriches our lives and fills us with satisfaction. Do not waste it, and keep in mind that all the good things in life take time. Let the people around you decide, in one way or another, to give you the most precious thing they have "time." Honor them and thank them for it.

Work is something that we all complain about, but it is what provides us with everything we have. All the great works involved arduous and extensive labor and continue to stand as enduring memories of civilizations that built their monuments, to bear witness to what can be achieved. It is admirable what can be achieved by working together as a team towards a common goal.

The Light That I Carry in Me

In reality, we want to earn a lot without putting in the necessary work. We must respect all work, as it is a form of art. There are hundreds of professions and tasks to choose from, so why complain? Let's simply look for what resonates most with us. Do not look down on any job; they are all important, and every person who does them deserves respect. I remember a time when people worked for free because they were eager to learn. They sought opportunities to improve themselves and were not concerned about how much they would earn. They understood that by learning, they could open doors to a better life.

I remember when I was young, between the ages of 11 and 16, my friends and I used to spend our school vacations learning different trades. I worked as a mechanic's assistant, a carpenter's assistant, a bricklayer's assistant, a loader of basic products in a market, and an assistant in an office supplies factory. These experiences taught me a lot about life and various professions, even though they were short-lived.

I was discovering what I really wanted to do with my life, and I am grateful for each job. Each one gave me different tools that, in one way or another, have helped me become the man I am today. I remember that, many times they paid us with lunch and a few bills, which was equivalent to 2 dollars for 5 days of work. But I felt like the wealthiest 11-year-old in the country.

At school, we often fail to appreciate the effort that teachers put into imparting the knowledge necessary for us to have better opportunities and grow into good individuals. Respect all your teachers, express gratitude to them, learn from them, and everything else will fall into place at the right time, when you are prepared for a blessing that demands a greater level of wisdom, skill, responsibility, and professionalism.

Fireproof Knights
NOTES

The Light That I Carry in Me

CHAPTER 10

⚜

Pay the Price

We all want to win and keep winning, but sometimes we refuse to pay the price necessary; to have a better life.

It is as if we expected a campfire to give us more heat without us putting a log of firewood inside it, it is illogical to expect from life without us to give and continue giving, we all want to receive, more and more, and we not only expect it, we demand it, and we feel indignant! With the right to complain, we feel that it is the world's obligation! That it is God's obligation! That it is someone's obligation to give us what we want!

Paying the price, is the best thing we can do, because by doing so, we enjoy the reward in a better way, we can feel proud because the prize was earned and not just given, because we are loved or because there are preferences towards us, or because we feel entitled by being related to the person in charge of the company, this mentality of entitlement is very dangerous, it can cost us a lot, especially when it can fill us with resentment and hatred if things are not resolved as we expect them.

Furthermore, we have to understand that sometimes the price to pay is just reading a book, being punctual and responsible at work, the price can be something as simple as it is difficult, *depending on what we are looking to receive in exchange, the price It can be years of effort and sacrifice, and even with that we are not guaranteed that we will obtain what we want with complete security!* **But** *In the end what we take with us is who we are becoming, because we have to consider that we are no longer the same, after exposing ourselves to a test, or a challenge; We will have gained experience and knowledge that will serve us forever, I can even tell you that every time we pay a price and acquire something in exchange, we are laying the foundations for a great life project in the future, but they are those small prices that we pay in a beginning, all those disciplines that we had to make part of our daily routine, all those sleepless nights studying for that final exam, all of that counts and you must appreciate yourself and congratulate yourself every time you reach an achievement, even if it seems insignificant. , celebrate it! And you will be motivated to get more.*

Many times, the price to pay is when we decide to say NO, to something that we really want, but we decide to sacrifice our fun, because we know that it is the only way, to have the time to prepare for the blessing. We decide to say no to parties, no to watching television, no to going out with friends, no to sleeping more, no to the food we like, because we know it is not good for us, and no to the comfort of our warm bed, to go to the gym to train, or get up super early to go to work, many times the price is saving, to be able to pay for a new talent that will give us greater income, the price can be attending seminars, or redesign workshops to know how to improve our life, sometimes, the price to Paying is simply taking action and taking a risk with the adventure of starting a business, which we have to make to work no matter what, but we know that no matter how long it takes for it to be successful, it is something that we are willing to do, to make it happen. For our dreams to come true, it is always worth

The Light That I Carry in Me

the effort, because the bigger the challenge, the prouder we will feel of having achieved it. Because if it were easy, anyone would do it, but if we are willing to pay whatever price is necessary to make our dreams come true, there will be no excuse, nor impediment to obtain our desires!

It is easy when there is a burning desire! Because the desire is so intense full of passion that for a moment doesn't allow you to have nothing else in your mind and heart moving you to take action with abandon and urgency.

If you have something that is calling you to act like this, that's a blessing! Believe that's possible and make it happen!

Fireproof Knights
NOTES

The Light That I Carry in Me

CHAPTER 11

⚜

What Do You Want from Life?

In one of the previous chapters, we discussed the importance of having a reason significant enough to fight for. In this chapter, we will discuss a topic that will inspire us to persevere and keep conquering each battle.

This time, we will focus on the experiences you want from life. What are your dreams? What are your goals? What is the one thing you desire to possess, that would bring you the utmost happiness and make you feel like the luckiest person in the world? What do you want that is worth the effort to do whatever it takes? Think of as many things as you can that inspire you to pay the price.

Have your own home.
Have a strong and toned body.
Live a dreamy romance with your loved one.
Be happy with your own decisions.
Stay in love with life.
Travel the world and get to see breathtakingly beautiful places.
Be a part of a foundation that helps children and families in need.
Have a business of your own.

Fireproof Knights

It's important to write down any dreams and goals you have, so that you can read them daily and carry them with you. This way when you feel like you need a little extra motivation, you can read them again!

Also, look for photographs and start by creating a vision board. Only include images of what you want to achieve in life, and select those that resonate with you. For example, if you aspire to be a doctor, include a cutout of a doctor. If possible, dress like one and have someone take a photo of you. Paste photos of your dream house and the places you would most like to visit— those that would bring you joy. Include images of a romantic life, the body you desire, and anything else that motivates you. Observe your vision board every day and express gratitude in advance, because one day, by the grace of God, it will manifest in your life.

It is important to consider the person you need to become in order to achieve your heart's desires. You must be willing to pay the price and work for your dreams. When they become a reality, they will be so beautiful that you will inspire many people to follow in your footsteps.

Remember that the primary goal is to grow and improve, to contribute and be part of something greater than ourselves, to leave a legacy where our actions are a subject of study and an example of perseverance and courage.

In the next chapters we will work very hard, and I promise you that there will be a lot of resistance, because in all of us there is something that is comfortable with the way things are, and is not interested in us changing in the slightest, it wants to deprive us of the opportunity to be what we are destined to be, since we arrived in the world; there are endless complexes, fears, excuses, bad

The Light That I Carry in Me

habits, beliefs, and all kinds of traps to keep us where we are. But we are not willing to continue being mediocre, we are going to fight to be the best version of ourselves. OK!
I AM GOING!

ARE YOU?

Just keep in mind in moments of doubt and fear that God is always with us, but this is something that needs to be done, we have to go through fire for our own good, when God grabs us by the hand he doesn't let us go, we grab God by the hand, we let go of him sometimes, but he never lets go of us, trust him and take action using your motivation tools and your reasons to fight and I assure you that we will emerge victorious, you will see.

AMEN.

Fireproof Knights
NOTES

The Light That I Carry in Me

CHAPTER 12

❦

The Base Is Love

At the end of a prayer, we always say AMEN, knowledge is available to everyone, but it is hidden in plain sight. What if the word amen wasn't simply a closing sentence? What if the word AMEN was the answer to our request? What if the response was so immediate, that it was given in advance because our need was already known ahead of time?

In Spanish the word amen can also mean to LOVE
When you love, everything is possible, where there is love there are blessings and miracles, so when we say AMEN, are we being invited to love? And to use LOVE as base.

A new commandment I give you: "That you love one another; As I have loved you, so you also love one another" When you love, everything is good, everything is enough, every effort is important, every word, every gesture, everything is valued and appreciated, and everything is blessed.

For a long time, I didn't know it, it's logical, but until it was revealed to me in a meditation, I understood everything so well, this is one of the greatest concepts and if you understand it in depth, you will realize that it is in everything that exist and

Fireproof Knights

will exist. It is a look beyond, a starting point to understand our history, our present and future. Because what lasts despite everything is LOVE! Love can do all things, and hopes all things, love never ceases to be, it continually transforms and transmutes. It comes when it has to, and it transforms, matures, and lasts. GOD is LOVE. And this is one identity of the FATHER.

When I say that the basis is love, I mean that you have to use a filter to discern any type of information, and go deep and look for the root. When there is love, what do you find? Health, happiness, peace, brotherhood, togetherness, and all kinds of positive emotions, because you can't curse or wish someone badly, when you have love in your heart. It is simply not possible. So, when you analyze something, someone, or a situation, look for the fruits of that root. If the fruits are negative: fear, imbalance, separation, frustration, anger, envy, resentment, poverty, etc. So, the basis is different.

Have you started to think about how in the Bible, which is a book of faith and hope and love, there is an apocalypse in it, like someone wanted to close the curtain on such beautiful work with fear, judgment, guilt, punishment, and torment? What is the basis for that? It's not love, then; Were tares sown amid the truth to confuse and create doubts? That way it keeps us warm. Between believing and not believing!
Between being and not being! Between light and darkness! Half believing.

The Light That I Carry in Me

Now with this, you can realize the intentions of everyone in this world, a curtain that covers your eyes from a truth is lifted, which if you practice and understand, will give you control of your life at all times, you will no longer be manipulable by nothing or anyone. Because if a person tells you that they are something and tells you about their intentions, but their fruits are something else, you already know that their basis is far from love.

What is the opposite of love?

We can understand that it is hatred, but I also feel the word fear in my heart, it is a word that we are taught, even in the same prayer with God, when we say fear of God, but I do not feel fear of him, for me, GOD is LOVE, what can make me afraid and frightened is his absence! The one who can no longer feel his presence. Even having failed so much, full of sins and lies, when I had the opportunity to be in his presence, what I felt was shame, never fear! I feel awe and reverence!

Because there are many other bases that we can use to achieve things in life, but their fruits are bitter and do not produce happiness, peace, or love.

For example, someone that's being hurt, now out of anger and resentment use that pain experience as fuel to succeed in life, and **might** *do whatever it takes to hurt back, to let people know that he, or she is successful and powerful but there is something in the inside that is hidden, the fear to be hurt again, so there is a shield that is impeding vibrate in a better frequency and allow love to find its way back, it is so hard to trust again, it is so difficult to* *experience a deep connection!*

The only good thing about this, would be to take a negative emotion, and use it to be successful, but what is not good is to continue carrying the emotion and punishing ourselves with it, by keeping it living inside us!

Sometimes we hurt other people because we were hurt, and it is not good; to manipulate or harm others either, to obtain a favorable result, or to payback, because one day the full weight of the truth will fall, and sadness, unhappiness and guilt, will be present.

There are feelings that apparently can lead us to success. But its end It is bitter as gall.
Do things out of hate.
For resentment.
For pride.
To get even.
For greed.
For spite.

For many reasons, any that prompts you to act is one of them, use your emotions, but don't let your emotions be used on you, acting for the wrong reasons can only produce the wrong fruits, and you will not enjoy your achievements, as you could. From a solid foundation such as love, and with this in no way, do I mean that you have to be something that you are not, or fake love, I mean there are many ways to show love, and in that frequency, we can find our way, love doesn't mean being soft and allow everyone to hurt us, we can have love in our hurts and be strong, full of character, brave but conscious of our strength, words and

The Light That I Carry in Me

actions.

In my case, by living with guilt, I wanted to compensate for my ills by being successful at my job, punishing myself, working more than 16 hours a day, without eating well and without enjoying life. I accumulated a lot of money and apparent happiness, but inside, I was feeling depressed. You, see? Guilt makes you bear fruit, and that way, you can achieve everything you set your mind to, but in the end if the foundation is not solid as a rock, any storm will destroy your sand castle.

Let God be your base, and with that love in you! You will achieve what you set your mind into, but it will be a path that you will enjoy better, because you will live in peace, you will feel good at all times and you will truly bear fruits sweet as honey, which will make That many people want to be like you, you will be recognized as a child of God and you will have the blessing of Father God in everything you propose.

Love what you do, love your neighbor, love everything in your life, but above all Love yourself!
But how?
But how can I sow from love, if I don't feel it in my heart? But how can I love after so much damage?
But how can I show love, if I was abused for so many years? How can I love again, if I gave everything away and they betrayed me like it was nothing?
How can I love, if my son died because of me?
How can I love if they abused me, when I was little? How can I love, if they abandoned me?

This part is very difficult and I understand you, I experienced a lot of it! I want

Fireproof Knights

you to:

On a blank page, write everything that prevents you from loving, but see more there and feel like is happening right now, revive the moment in your head and feel it, show the emotion, do not Repress any feelings! What do you feel?
Hate, shout it...
I hate you I hate you I hate you....... I hate you ....
I hate you, because I trusted you and you deceived me.......
I hate you because you left me alone.......
I hate myself because I didn't fight for your love...
I hate you because you used me..........
I hate you because you abused me..........
I hate you mom because you didn't believe me.............
I hate you dad because I was never enough for you....
I hate you sister, because you never loved me...
I hate you brother because you hit me when I was little....
I hate you man because you abused me....
I hate you because you left me with nothing....
I hate you God because, I always believed in you and where were you when they were raping me? Where?

I know that remembering is hard, it is difficult and it is not for cowards, even if it is not your time to express what you feel, wait, there is no rush, it is on your time, only you

You know what you have inside, I just want to tell you that you are not alone. And you are not the only person who has experienced something like this, some people go through life with a mask that everything is fine when they are broken inside, full of hate and resentment, fears, doubts, insecurities, and demands are made on us. Equally, as a person who has had everything and has suffered nothing. I know it's unfair, and I'm not here to convince you otherwise.

The Light That I Carry in Me

I understand you perfectly, it is not easy, but it is the way to go. Take your time, and relive everything again, person by person, situation by situation, and bring out that hate that you have inside. Hate is like saying: I love you, "it is an emotion" you have to express it, the person does not have to be present, nor does anyone else. Just you alone or with someone to accompany you. As you decide, you can shout it, you can write it all and then burn it, you can talk about it in a conversation, you can relive it in your mind, and express your feelings with tears, with anger, however, you want to express it at the moment you want, whenever you want, without anyone knowing.

The energy that is trapped will disappear in the same way, the problems in your stomach will disappear because the chemical of hate will be released and will no longer be able to poison your body. You will see the results quickly and you will be ready to continue in your process.

This Path Without a Doubt, Is for The Brave!

I LOVE YOU & Thank YOU for taking a chance on YOU!

Fireproof Knights

The Light That I Carry in Me

CHAPTER 13

⚜

Forgiveness is The Way

After expressing our feelings, it is best to allow ourselves to accept forgiveness as a stone where we can build a new beginning. The vast majority of the time, we refuse to work on forgiveness and decide to carry this for many years, even an entire life, thinking that the people who hurt you do not deserve your forgiveness, and perhaps they do not deserve it, especially when they do not even ask for it. They have not even repented, but the good is for you! The healing is for you! And what you let go benefits you!

But what happened if, I don't feel it?

Just repeat, I forgive you, I forgive you; even without feeling it up to 70 times 7, daily, constantly, whenever it comes to your thoughts say "I FORGIVE YOU".

And if you are the cause of a lot of harm, ask for forgiveness from the bottom of your heart and repeat to yourself: "I FORGIVE MYSELF", even if you don't feel it, in the same way 70 times 7. (490 times)

I guarantee that, if you do, little by little you will remove the callousness from your heart and forgiveness will be more honest and healing, and over time your heart will not hold any type of resentment and forgiveness will be instantaneous.

But we are so used to being judges, to judging others and judging ourselves severely, that we will remember a failure for life. It doesn't have to be like this, "GOD HAS ALREADY FORGIVEN YOU; NOW FORGIVE YOURSELF." The beautiful thing about all this is that you can transmute any feelings through forgiveness.

And if you really feel sorry. Take action and begin to bear the fruit of forgiveness. Be different, help others, find a way to give back in gratitude for the forgiveness obtained. If they forgive you, forgive, and if you seek forgiveness, first forgive all faults, "giving is how we receive"

Asking for forgiveness, doesn't make you less or more. It simply puts you on a better frequency, to continue moving forward in life! Because through lack of forgiveness, you can get stuck in a fragment of the past. And it is not fair, because you did not come into this world to live paying for a mistake, nor to live blaming for a failure.

JUST FORGIVE!

The way in which it is easier for me, to take this step is by remembering that: "we do not know what we are doing", most of the time, many times we offend without knowing it, without realizing it, and when we do it being conscious, our guilt bother us and doesn't Let us continue, it makes us uncomfortable every time we touch the subject.

The Light That I Carry in Me

Repeat, "I forgive you: _____because you didn't know what you were doing,

"If you really knew the damage you were doing to me, you wouldn't have done it"

This, for me, gives me comfort, provides the benefit of the doubt for the other person and, above all, puts you in a state of compassion, and ultimately "Liberates you" and that is the purpose: liberation, why do you want to continue? Carrying something that prevents you from being happy?

Forgive me, because I did not know what I was doing. If I had known the harm, I was doing to you, I would never have hurt you, because there is not a day that I do not have remorse and guilt. Forgive me, free me too, please!

This is what I repeated, with tears asking for forgiveness, alone in my room. And I felt forgiven by God and the other person and then I constantly repeated to myself: "I forgive myself," until I felt forgiven."

And then I focused on giving fruits of forgiveness, fruits of mercy, fruits of gratitude, fruits of joy and fruits of love for the forgiveness received.

It's your turn to take action, don't think about it, act. I assure you that you will find the peace that so many are looking for.

It's time to free ourselves!

Fireproof Knights

The Light That I Carry in Me

Do not judge

One of the habits that helped me the most to free myself from an exaggeratedly large emotional burden was to no longer judge. It was a bit difficult for me not to do it, but I saw in other people flaws, moments of weakness, "sins", failures, cowardice, injustice, etc. And since I was little, I was under the influence of people indoctrinated in a religion, where I learned the hard way, to believe that I had to be perfect, at all times, and to criticize those who had failed.

And I don't want to say that religion is bad or the people who participate in it, everything has a reason for existing, and in my case, it was that way, regularly when we were children, we imitated everything, without even receiving a logical explanation of why it has to be like that, in that way. We just obeyed and, woe! If I didn't obey at that time, when I was a child, what a beat up waiting for me!

So, we create an image that we must behave in a certain way, and when we fail, we feel very bad. I remember, one time I was very hungry, I was a little kid, maybe 6 years old, and I remember they had hidden some bananas on top of the refrigerator, for one of my uncles' breakfasts, and well, it was already night and I put a chair to reach a banana, I grabbed it and ate it. After a moment; I felt so bad, because I had stolen; I spent many nights afterwards asking God for forgiveness, because I didn't want to go to hell.

And I think this story is just a reflection of what adults sometimes do. With our children, we yell at them, we lie to them *and we severely correct them, so that they are good men and women according to our irrational thinking, we make them believe that they have to be perfect and we cause such great damage to them, without even realizing it, since That moment we have taught them to judge others, to criticize and point out all the defects and errors in others, and this is how our attitude is formed as a judge and as a wrongdoer.*

Now, I understand perfectly that: what we see in others is, what we must work on ourselves! That is the reason of what others do, makes us so angry. It causes us endless thoughts and judgments. Prisoners of customs and traditions that prevent us from having the energy necessary to move forward.

We have to stop doing it and if we catch ourselves doing it, let's start again, let's not judge ourselves either, because the person we owe the most, that freedom, is us. We have to get out, of the prison where we find ourselves, don't we realize, how much energy we waste in judging?... "Too much."

It is not worth it, and often when we judge, we do not know all the details of the matter to make a correct decision when rendering a judgment.

In addition, in the same Bible we are told: "let us not judge so, that they do not judge us." So many reasons not to do it, but in an oversight, we go back to this bad habit. It's like we're all programmed to see one defect among 99 qualities.

When we don't judge, we release that energy that consumes a lot of our life and our time, and best of all, we put ourselves in a state of peace, where what others do, is no longer of interest to us. If we let go of what's extra, the path will be more pleasant.

The Light That I Carry in Me

For every time our mind leads us, to judge someone, set ourselves the task of finding two positive things about the same person. When we want to judge ourselves, let's spend some time in front of the mirror and look into our eyes and repeat to ourselves some achievements we have done and some qualities we have. Little by little our self-esteem will grow more and more, and we will feel better and blessed for the wonderful beings that we are.

Don't Compare Yourself

One of the main reasons why we blind ourselves and cannot appreciate what we have is when we compare ourselves to others, in a negative way.
That the other person is taller, thinner. Prettier than me.
Who has the hair that I would like to have. The skin color is beautiful, not like mine. Who has a car and I don't.
who has a partner and I'm still alone, why? If she is uglier than me, and we use phrases like: "the pretty ones desire the fate of the ugly."
When we stop for a moment and pay attention, to this way of acting, it really makes us sad and we can only have compassion, because in that state of mind, we focus so much on others that we completely forget about ourselves and to enjoy our life!

You know, everything you see in others is in you too. It is good to appreciate the beauty and good in others, it is beautiful and it is healthy. The only problem with it is when we use it to attack ourselves, that I don't have this, or that, then we put ourselves in a state of constant complaint and comparison; and we despise our person. Let's appreciate what we have and little by little we will find more and more reasons to give thanks.

We all have something special and unique, but we haven't discovered it yet, and that makes us notice other people and admire them.

But the reality is, you are special and wonderful, more so in the eyes of God, find your value, find your talent, don't try to have the same life and the same experiences as someone else, just because you think that will make you feel better. Discover what makes you happy, look only at your happiness.

I remember: when I made my vision board, I was looking for images of things that I wanted to obtain in my life, I put the image of a Lamborghini, just because the person who was being my guide at that moment, loved a life of luxury and exotic things, and I didn't want her to think that I was satisfied with little. I gave up what I really liked because I wanted to be like someone else. I compared my life for a long time, with all the people who were around me, and it was ugly, because I felt bad, when this or another person was doing better than me, but I was a little happy, if I was better than this one, or another person. Now I can only think of all the time I wasted, with an attitude like that.

Many times, even having my own business! I felt very disappointed at me, because I spoke to someone who told me "I already have 2 restaurants", so in my mind, instead of thanking God, for having the possibility of having my own business, the comparison came and I told myself, "Marlon, you're staying behind, look he has two restaurants and you only one"... and so

The Light That I Carry in Me

on with everything: that he has brand name shoes and you don't, that the clothes are designer brand and yours not, his car is better than yours, the house is nicer, and you still renting. In short, this is something that we have to leave behind, not only because of the tinges of envy, that comes to light, but also because we tend to forget that, we all have the opportunity to be more and have more! But not through comparison used in a negative way. "That is not the way".

It is different when we use healthy comparison, where we are happy for the successes of others and use that as an impulse, thinking: "if this person can have this or that, why couldn't I have it?"

So, it becomes a type of competition where we have those people we admire and pay more attention to:
How did they get it?
What habits do they have?
What do they read?
What do they do?
What don't they do?
What mentality do they have?
How did they get to, where they are right now?
Who do I have to become, to get what I want?
What kind of person do I have to be, to attract the right person into my life?
How do I get to, where I want to go?
Could it be that this person, who already got what I want, could give me advice?
Can they give me a clue?

Regularly, a person who is already having success in life, what they want most is to help others to reach the next level, so as not to *feel like they are alone, and also feel that one can make a difference in a positive way in the world of someone else's life! And this is something that is priceless, is a blessing to be able to help others!*

"Do not compare yourself, you are a unique being, with unique talents, God made you the way you are for a reason, an invaluable treasure is hidden in you, find it and share it with the world."

"Let's ask God to shine His light into our hearts, helping us see Him clearly"

The Light That I Carry in Me
CHAPTER 14

⚜

Let go and trust

How many times we ask for help, and since we see that it takes a while, or it is done in a different way than what we have in mind, we decide it is better to do it ourselves. This is a bad habit that prevents us from being able to trust other people. It puts burdens on us that are unnecessary, prevents help from arriving, and makes others give up wanting to help us. Either because they see that we do not give them the opportunity and full confidence to take control of the situation, or also because we do not give them the opportunity to learn, and the only way to learn is through trying and correcting and trying again. Until we achieve it; It takes time, we have to let go and trust.

How many times do we ask God for help, and then when things start to move in a way that we don't know, it generates doubts, fears, and we want to get involved, when what God is doing is working for us. God will always want the best for us, but we have to trust him and let go of the outcome. God can see the future, the present and the past, while we cannot even see the blessings that are right in front of our nose.

When it comes from God, it is felt, things begin to flow in a different way. Just take a moment and really see if what is happening is based on love, or is it another emotion that is based on, because this stone will be used to build a fortress, or a sand castle.

Fireproof Knights

I know that trust is difficult, especially when we have suffered many betrayals, but today I tell you, do not change your essence, or who you are inside, stay authentic, keep shining, illuminating the lives of others!

Once upon a time, there was a businessman called Or, who gave a small merchant an opportunity to talk to him about a project, with his sights set on a partnership! But before talking about business, or told him: brother, I want to ask you a question, what defect do you think you need to remove from yourself? For me it is important to know, what am I facing when entering into a partnership with you. The merchant called Avad, took a deep breath, he knew that the answer could somewhat affect his business relationship, after about 15 seconds, Avad responded: Friend Or, my biggest flaw is that: I am very trusting, and I have lost many times, to people who have taken advantage of me. I would like to get rid of that defect forever!

You know, friend Avad, precisely what you call a defect is what caught my attention to do business with you, it is very difficult to find a person who has good will, and who always expects the best from others, who trusts others, the way you do it. You expect the best from others and that, my friend, is what gives me peace of mind and inspires me to trust! Because I know that is what you have inside, you are full of love, compassion, security and good principles, that just by being by your side makes me feel peaceful and thankful.

When I heard this story, I felt like it vibrated with me, because like Avad I am too trusting at times, I have lost many times, but now, I understand that it was a blessing! Because the people who hurt us, who use us, who borrow from us and don't pay us! They walk away alone! And little by little we are left alone, next to real

The Light That I Carry in Me

and honest people, like us. The tares separate themselves from the chaff and it ends up being burned! We will have what we lost again because we know how to get it back, while the person who took it from us will always have lack, scarcity and will close all the doors on his own, and has to constantly start over, and as the years go by; that person will continue to be in the same place or a place below.

I have a friend who I love very much, and I asked her these 2 questions: The first was:
What would you like to let go?
Knowing the answer, I asked her the following:
Why do you feel that, what you want to let go of, is a weakness?

Her answer to the first question was: "I am very sensitive, I cry a lot, I don't want to be like that anymore."
The answer to the second question was: "It's just that all the people, by seeing that I am very sensitive, want to take advantage of me, they talk loudly to me, they even yell at me, and all I do is start crying, because I don't know how to react otherwise."

Upon knowing this, I noticed! That something happened to her when she was little; and she herself later confirmed it to me! I know that it is not easy, and many of us have gone through such unpleasant things, we keep memories that constantly torment us, and we have gone through situations that marked us, we feel useless at times and that we have no control over our way of being and reacting, and we focus on holding on to the fact that we are made in this way and that's it. We can all let go, but we have to know how to let go, because when I see my friend, she seems like a person so tender, so kind, with such a beautiful heart, there are always positive and kind words when referring to others!

Fireproof Knights

I know that one or another person, who has been damaged by some type of abuse has become insensitive! Will focus their gaze on my friend, because she has something that is an opposite reflection of what they are not, for other people my friend may seem like a weak person, and they can't stand her being the way she is, and they treat her in a harsh way, thinking that they are doing her a favor, whether consciously or unconsciously; and that by being harsh will help her, so that she becomes strong, they are people who carry in their mind "that this world is a hard place, where only strong people survive", and as it is in their mind, that is their reality.

On the other hand, my friend thinks she has to change because she thinks; consciously or unconsciously, that "being a sensitive person makes you weak and subject to abuse," and just as you believe it, you create it.

For me, we have to let go of the way we focus on something, because although we try to work on certain points that make us "vulnerable, or insensitive", we can find a balance between both and at the same time use our way of being to favor us and not to go against us, for example, if I am a person like my friend: sensitive, loving and compassionate; I can work in a job where people with these qualities are required, for example: teacher, nurse, social worker, or I can focus my sensitivity towards writing, painting or a different sort of art or sport. Maybe it is difficult for me to express my feelings when I feel attacked, but I can let go and understand that the person attacking me is really the one asking for help, so I shouldn't take it personal and have a conversation if possible and express my disapproval on what I don't like and always try to improve the social interaction with the focus

The Light That I Carry in Me

on reaching an agreement!

Sometimes we need a new point of view, maybe we are not seeing clearly, and we need a different perspective to be able to find a solution that makes us feel better, and useful by the way we are. Because we do not have to confuse our essence with the way we react to life, we can ask God for wisdom and discernment! If we have doubts between what we should let go of, and what we should look at with different eyes! Many times, what we have to let go of, it is the place where we are, maybe we don't feel valued, we feel attacked by our way of being, by our essence; If so, a change is necessary! By being in the wrong place, we will never be what we are destined to be, it is as if we planted roses in the desert, or palm trees in the snow, it is very complicated to adapt and even more giving our best, standing out and shining, would be too exhausting of a task. Let's do ourselves a favor, and let's look for the environment that best suits us, don't fool ourselves to the idea that we have to be in a place, because that's what we have to do, and that's it, let go of that idea too.

When we have been doing the same thing for a long time, and we are already bored, every day is a regret, and we don't let go because we have convinced ourselves that we are that what we do! And we can't do anything else! When the human being has within him the possibility of becoming anyone that decides to be, and learn anything that has decided to learn, all we have to do is:

pay the price!

If we know that we are not happy, why not let go of the mask of happiness, why pretend to be something that we are not, if we are not, let's try to be, I believe this is the bravest thing we can do, because it requires leaving the mold imposed by us or others!

Fireproof Knights

Being happy is not an answer that interests everyone, many are more interested in having and possessing everything material that can exist, even if in the inside there is an existential void that is very difficult to fill up. It is because we are searching to answer the call in our soul to find our true meaning in life, that we will fill that we don't belong there will be conflict with people around us, very few will understand us, and many fewer, will support us, because they will not understand, the courage to go for what we love, and for what makes us happy, even at the risk of being alone! But then again, I tell you, it is no one's fault! There are no culprits, it is the programming that makes us accept or reject, a life protocol, and since seeking for true happiness, is outside of the established pattern, it receives rejection, but with the passage of time and the awakening of consciousness; the new trend will be to seek to be happy and live in peace, in a more conscious and sensitive world for the well-being of everyone, as part of the same world.

We have to put our trust in God, and trust in the process, let go little by little of everything that does not contribute to our life, bad habits, bad thoughts, bad desires, people who are taking advantage of us, people who at this moment, don't have to be in our life, change may be slow, but deep in my heart, I assure you that you know, that you are walking in the right way.

We, also need to let go, is when we are distressed, when we feel anxious about the future, when things are not clear; moments of doubt exist in all people, sometimes we do not show it, but most of us at times, do not know what we are doing! But it is in these moments, when it is necessary to trust God, knowing that one way or another everything will turn out well, but here the secret is: TAKE ACTION, in what it is up to us to do, and let's leave to God what it is up to Him to do.

The Light That I Carry in Me

Let's not worry about what is to come and let's make the most of the now, in itself, it is the only time that exists, even when we remember something from the past; we relive it in the now, something from the future, we also see it in the now. There is only this "now" moment.

Attachment is something that, at this stage of our life, when we want to let go, it will be constantly be present. I know that it is difficult, that it hurts, and that it is very, very hard to let go, but it is the only way to really see, that it is not healthy, because we are not supposed to have any attachment to anything, or anyone; because it is a perception of our ego, which makes us believe, that we need something or someone, and it is not like that! We have to be free, to actually be able to discover our potential, and what we are capable of, we must be free to experience life in abundance, and trust that God will help us every step of the way.

Trust in yourself! It is incredible what human beings are capable of doing, we have enormous potential, and there are practically no limits to what we can create, the only thing we always have to remember is that the basis must be love, with love and for love, whatever we decide to do, will be worth the effort and will be something that as the years go by, will fill us with pride and satisfaction and not only us, but also to God.

The word "let go" does not mean, wait for everything to resolve itself and for God to do miracles for us, we have all the tools we need to do our part, all we have to do, is feel in our heart, what feelings it causes us? When thinking about something specific Is it? Frustration! Anger! Sadness! Or any negative emotion! That's what we should let go! Even a dream or a goal can make us start feeling frustrated and anxious when not getting achieved, it is *better to let go as well of those feelings and look for another way to approach at what we want! We can have the goal or dream very present, and do what is necessary and what it is in our hands but let go of the outcome! Which in time will be achieved by a change of habits, the implementation of a system and the processes created to attain what we want.*

If something has not come into our life, it means that it is not yet the time, either for reasons beyond our control, or because we haven't made it happen, we have to be honest and discern why? We don't have to wait for the perfect moment, but we can wait for the right moment for us and then take action with intention and determination to go for that one desire!

Let Go of what's not helping us and trust God, with Him by our side:
All things are possible!

The Light That I Carry in Me

CHAPTER 15

❧

Look for the good in everything

It is a tendency for many to always focus on the bad, and we do it constantly. Thank God, negative energy is not part of our nature, and that is why the bad takes much longer to materialize, but it happens and then when it arrives, takes us by surprise! Yeah, right! If we have been calling it all the time, with our words and actions.

We wait for bad news to happen, mothers worry, when their children arrive a little later than usual, expecting the worst. A new boss arrives, with new ideas for the company, we think for sure they are going to start laying off staff. A husband takes a little longer at work, he's probably cheating on.

We tend to focus our attention, on people's defects and we get involved in mini conflicts at work, school, home, in the neighborhood, on the bus, when driving the car, everywhere. We get engaged in absurd fights, that take away our peace and distract us, from what really matters: OUR HAPPINESS! The worst of all is that; many times, we find ourselves fighting over something so simple! That is ridiculous, perhaps we have been carrying something internally, and by fighting with someone for whatever, "we release that pressure a little, and that makes us feel a little bit better."

There are many ways to look at it, and I can guarantee that we all suffer from this bad habit, whether to a lesser or greater extent. So, what happens? It deprives us of many opportunities for growth! Steals opportunities from us, injects us with pessimism, and distances us from the peace of our being.

Looking for the good in everything is the solution. It is so logical, and easy when everything is going well, but when things are not turning out as we expect it, is difficult to maintain a positive thought.

It's worth the effort, yes of course! Like everything, one step at a time, remember that you are fighting with programming that is hundreds of years old. It is common and normal, although it is not what suits us, because in us we find a creative power, so powerful that each of us has the ability, to transform a heaven into a hell, and a hell into a heaven.

Use the benefit of the doubt, when rumors of bad things arrive, remain neutral! And little by little control your mind, and incline your thinking; to a tone of positivity. This will keep you in control of the situation, and improve your reaction to adversity.

Our peace of mind it is so important, we have to guard our mind, all the time! So that we can vibrate high, and have the energy to realize all our dreams, and goals and that should be our focus. Don't be preoccupied, don't pre-occupied our mind with things ahead, creating mental movies of the possible outcome, especially if we can't do anything about it!

I used to have the habit of watching the news at night, while having dinner. It was a ritual that we faithfully repeated day after day, without knowing that we were unconsciously

The Light That I Carry in Me

programming ourselves to expect bad news. And although it is true that some news had a positive tone, the vast majority always contained airs of hopelessness, sadness, cruelty, violence, extortion, etc. It is even worse! When we are programmed to these types of realities, at a very tender age, because we have no defenses, we do not question, we are easy to educate for good, or bad! According to the convenience of the protocol that is taught.

But now it is our decision to plant a different seed in our mind, we control what comes into our family. What kind of life do we want to have? Don't you think it's worth it? To let go of the bad and focusing only, on what can bring: light, love, kindness, hope, happiness and the achievement of our goals and dreams.

We have to make an effort and be brave, because, depending on our approach to the good, we will see miracles happen in our life and in the lives of others. See the good in yourself, don't focus on your flaws, we all have them, but the secret is to accept them and make the best of what we are and have, this will make you a confident person with healthy self-esteem.

Look for the good in others, by doing this not only do we make them feel better, but we also create bonds of friendships and brotherhood that will make our life more pleasant.

Flaws, we all have! I remember as a child, we had nicknames for everyone, it was fun to notice some detail in a friend, and bother him with it, but it was even, so we didn't see it as bad. It made us strong! At that age it was what I believed! But we innocently undermined our self-esteem. Now I consciously laugh at those nicknames and share with my kids' stories about how original or ordinary they were. Children's things! Which created bonds of brotherhood and memories that I will remember all my life with nostalgia.

By focusing on the good, miracles happen, we see paths where there were none, we see hope where there was none, we attract rain into the desert. You can become such a nice person, so that it will be really nice to share the same space for the light that shines within, and that's what this world needs, people who are willing to contemplate a different way of walking thru life!

We have to do our part day by day, we just need to be aware of our thoughts, feelings and emotions, it is easy, because if they make us feel good, we are on the right track, if they make us feel bad, then we need to correct the signal we are sending so nothing comes back to us, that "we don't want".

At first, we will have to be very aware, but then our brain begins to assimilate that it is our new way of thinking, feeling and acting and begins to do it on autopilot. And when we get to that moment everything flows easily, without effort. Remember, we are not alone!

There are many of us who want a better future for ourselves, and our children. Step by step, winning battle after battle, evil will not be able to defeat good.

Thanks for believing!

The Light That I Carry in Me
CHAPTER 16

❧

The Truth About Money

The truth is that money is a tool, and you have to start seeing it as such. Many people go through life chasing more and more money, after they achieve the amount, they set for themselves, what do you think happens? They keep increasing it, we set a higher goal and we are caught in that trap again and again. When would be enough?

Money helps us, but we always have to have a balance, if we have little, we can't enjoy anything in life, and we will be continually stressed by the lack of it, and we tend to look for something or someone to blame for our "bad luck." If we have a lot, without having the ability to use it, in a healthy and responsible way, our life will become complicated, we will not live peacefully, we may desire more and more, but we will not take advantage of it. Because money amplifies the type of person we already are; If we are generous, we will be more generous, if we are arrogant, we will be more so, if we like to humiliate others, with more money we will believe, that we have the right to do it, even more!

The important thing is, that we are using it as a tool, exchanging it for experiences; that enrich our life, because at the end: the material things remain. So, there's no point in having too much, if we are not going to enjoy it.

Fireproof Knights

Living in abundance! Not only refers to money, but also love, health, personal relationships, family moments, experiences, all of this counts as part of our fortune, and that's what we will be enjoying later, all those memories!

What I can tell you is: as a first, we have to appreciate what we have, even if we only have a little, then we have to add the habit of saving and looking for ways to save some more, the next thing is: we have to spend less, by being aware of what we really need! And then look for ideas on how to earn more, and of course apply them! We don't have to be afraid to invest in ourselves, the more money we move intelligently by investing it in skills, that help us become better, the more we position ourselves to earn more. We have to be smart and learn to manage our wealth with care and integrity. It is very important to avoid impulse purchases and reducing unnecessary spending Don't worry or fall into the trap of making money quickly and easily, that doesn't have a solid foundation, and it's not just about making money in whatever! It's better if we first find what is it, that we are passionate about, and then work on it. If we do this, in time we will have the experience, and the ability to do more with our talent.

Detach ourselves from money, for many it is difficult to let go, but giving is how we receive! What we give is what we receive, trust in time, do not be dazzled by false prophets who tell us to accompany them, promising a life of richness and false happiness, in the end there is emptiness, I have witnessed many people who manage to have incredible amounts of money, but the price for it, has been too high! And in the end, it was not worth it!

There are people who have decided to help, even if they don't have a lot, but they understand that there are people who are

The Light That I Carry in Me

suffering; and by doing so, the doors of opportunity tend to open wide for them, bringing more opportunities and more abundance to their lives!

He who complains about money will always have more reasons to continue complaining, and he who blesses and appreciates it, will have money multiplied and will have it in abundance! We always have to control money, don't let money control us!

Make our goal to have plenty, but not because of the amount of money, rather because of the type of person we have to become to achieve it, what new habits we have to acquire and what habits we have to let go.

Money is a blessing when used correctly! And not only will we achieve all our dreams and goals, also we have the possibility of helping many people in need around the world, we can also donate our time, or our knowledge! It is thanks to the good use of money and resources that we are able to achieve an extraordinary life, surrounded with wonderful people and amazing experiences!

Money can and should help us, as a tool of exchange, for what we need at each stage of our life, money is a facilitator!

If we Value and, if we are grateful, for every penny we have, our relationship with money be improved! For money has a particular frequency and if we learn to appreciate its presence, we will have more, if on the contrary, we constantly complain that everything is expensive and that we don't have enough for more, having money with us will be something negative, so we unconsciously be pushing it away, rejecting it. Money has an energy that can be used to do good and bad, we give it the work we consider correct. We can spend it, or invest it, we can use it, or be used by it. If we *think about it! The truth is: "we don't use having so much money to live well and in abundance" we just need to learn:" to manage it better, to get the most out of it"*

We have to have control over ourselves, so as not to waste it on things that have no value, it is very easy to fall into the trap of pretending, what is fashionable is to boast of a lifestyle that we do not really have, to screen and make believe that we are something we are not. Social networks are a very powerful tool, and they have a lot of force to suggest to many, their use would have to be responsible, because whether through malice or ignorance we can cause harm or be harmed; "with great power, great responsibility", and we were not prepared for this, it was from one moment to the next, where technology took over our lives, but not for the correct purposes in most of the times, rather because of the money that is involved.

It is incredible how the middle class is disappearing, there are many people living in poverty, full of shortages in things that should be easier to acquire, and we have millionaires accumulating too much money, spending it on unnecessary things. Financial education plays a fundamental role in modern society, to know how to make the right decisions with money! We have to pay the price, to be better prepared and prepare our future generations, and as always, assume responsibility for where we are financially, not blame anyone or anything, stop envying and wish evil on those who have a lot, rather learn from them the good, the bad we have to discard it, and understand that we only know such a small percentage of the truth, which is why we should not allow ourselves to judge any person, regardless of whether they have a lot of money or little.

Bless the money whenever it comes to us, so that the energy that

The Light That I Carry in Me

comes with it, is transmuted! Give thanks when receive it and when give it; Bless it! So, wherever it arrives carries an energy of prosperity and abundance!

The good intention we place, when having contact with money it's enough, we have to put it to good use, and it will come back amplified! Never feel distressed by the lack of money, because this will make us have anxiety and since that is a very strong negative emotion, it will make the money go away, so that we feel more and more anxious and distressed and the lack of money prevail, so that's the worst thing you can do.

The best thing is not to tell anyone when we are in an uncomfortable situation, where we are tight due to the absence of money, the best thing is to pray in secret and ask God for a source of income, for an idea, for a job, for an opportunity, and at once! Look for it, take action and take steps of faith, don't wait for a miracle in a rested position, better actively participate, and change the situation we are in!

We are the miracle! We can be that angel of light for someone else, especially if we help those who cannot return the favor! We can give hope, if we set our mind to it, we can show the way, when we discover it! When we learn! When we heal!

Today I want to give thanks for all the money that I have had! I give thanks for all the money that I have in this moment! I give thanks from where it comes from, and to where it goes! And I bless all money that my hands touch, in the name of *I Am That, I Am*.

Fireproof Knights
NOTES

The Light That I Carry in Me

CHAPTER 17

❦

Give Thanks for Everything, At Every Moment!

This is one of my favorite chapters, because everything good in life begins to happen in a very different way when we are grateful. It is the root of abundance, happiness and peace!

Since we are little, we are taught to give thanks; but we do it in a way that is not so profound, as the years go by, in a somewhat superficial way, we say thank you. Perhaps out of habit, out of politeness, out of respect, to show that we have good manners, to please our parents and family, so that they feel proud of us for being polite.

When in reality what we have to do is to give thanks from the bottom of our hearts for everything. Also, for what we think it is bad! There are endless reasons to be grateful, but many times we go entire days without feeling gratitude.

It is important to take the time to start doing it. This habit will help us be prepared for more and better things. If there is something I have discovered, it is that before having more we must be grateful for what have at this very moment! Otherwise what we have, however little, will be taken from us, changing hands to someone who truly values and understands this principle!

How do babies or small children appreciate? By completely enjoying what they are given! A caress, a kiss, a hug, our time. And in return they give us wonderful smiles, laughter or displays of affection so sweet and tender that they melt our hearts.

Let us be like children, let us be more present in the now and enjoy everything that is constantly given to us for free, the rays of the sun, a beautiful sunset, the rain, the wind, the water and its freshness, our food, love. Of our loved ones, we go through the world wanting to achieve so many material things when what really matters is what we already have.

Our health is one of those things, we couldn't do absolutely nothing without having health. We already gave thanks for that? We do not have to wait for something; to no longer be there, to begin to appreciate it! I know that "we were not taught that way", but it is our responsibility now to constantly improve, correct and learn, so that we are in harmony with the new frequency in which we are thinking about being part of.

There are many techniques to practice gratitude, but for me the best thing is to give ourselves at least 5 minutes in the morning when we wake up and simply breathe deeply, becoming aware of what a new day means, and of all the opportunities we have, by being alive one more day.

Before going to sleep, take at least 10 minutes to review what we did during the day, give thanks for the beautiful moments, give thanks for the difficult moments, but change the vibration of them and repeat them in our mind in the way we would have liked to happened. Never go to sleep angry, sad, or feeling a negative

The Light That I Carry in Me

emotion, instead we focus our attention on giving thanks for those moments of our life we want more of, if necessary, bring out a fond memory that can put a smile to your face, could be a happy moment lived with loved ones, an achievement or a fun experience. With eyes closed take a few deep breaths, and visualize the memory in vivid details; trying to engage all the senses, smell, touch, what you heard, what you saw, tasted and felt, with the intention to feel again the same experience, and then just stay for as long as possible feeling that sensation of happiness, joy, bliss until you are ready to open your eyes, at last is just necessary to reflect and be thankful knowing that we are able to revisit that happy moment whenever we need a boost.

I give thanks to God for everything I have experienced in the past, and that makes me realize that: I am blessed for having a new opportunity to do what I love, for having food on my table, for having clean water to drink. Being present and truly enjoying and savoring what life has to offer is the best way to express gratitude! I love food and I love cooking, being grateful for this, it is not difficult for me.

When having the opportunity to give a hug, a caress or a kiss! Let's give it with a different meaning, making love not to seek gratification, or remove an impulse that makes us uneasy, but truly give thanks to our loved ones for their time, honor them and show them love, feeling the warmth and energy, the rhythm of the heartbeat, being grateful for it and feeling like suddenly, everything takes on a different tone, a magical tone, a special shine, suddenly everything is better, and there is no need for nothing more.

It is beautiful to enjoy every moment of the day, at dusk, to give thanks and fall asleep with that feeling in our hearts. It is such a beautiful thing to live life in a state of continuous gratitude, without a doubt, we are ensuring with this a beautiful future for ourselves.

And when we put ourselves in a state like that, everything conspires to get to us. Just like when we give a gift, and it is welcomed, and appreciated that the desire is to give more, and keep on giving!

There are people who can fake gratitude to receive things, they are fooling themselves, because maybe they can say thank you, but if we pay attention, they don't really mean it. And it is sad when universal laws are used for convenience, to obtain something, "giving to receive is not giving, but rather taking" When the true nature of everyone and everything is: "Give and Share."

Because if what we are doing is taken away, sooner or later it will be taken away from us, and it will not be a little, "It will be more than expected."

And it's not about repeating thank you everywhere in vain. Feel the gratitude, live it and your blessings will be multiplied, you will have so much that you can share. Just remember to take into account each area of your life, and you will see how all those areas will prosper.

The Light That I Carry in Me

CHAPTER 18

⚜

My love

When we think about Love, we always think about someone else! When the first person we have to dedicate our love and honor to, is ourselves! It is very clear in a commandment: "Love your neighbor as yourself." But if we don't love ourselves, how can we truly love someone else? Maybe we do it, but in reality, not as it should be, we settle for giving half-hearted love and half-receiving, we even think; that love is not necessary, that we can live without it.

Many times, we get confused, because we have a need for love, and we do not understand that need and we want to fill it in one way or another, but we have to understand that there are many kinds of love: Love for God, our family, our friends, pets, places, ourselves, love for that special person in our lives.

There are so many types of love that we can experience, they are there to provide us with energy and motivation for everything we decide to do, we just have to look for that energy, or better yet, surround ourselves with every type of love as part of our daily lives, so we will have our tanks full, at all times!

My mission in life with my children is to be there for them! But it doesn't matter what decision they decide to make, I know would be the right one, because it will be based on love, and not because of ego, fear, revenge.

Sometimes the need, of an absent parent marked us, so that it fills our heart with resentment, or we tend to seek love out of necessity! As I once did! Wanting to fill a void, which is only filled for a brief moment, and the need returns and forces us to look for another momentary patch! And this causes us to enter a cycle where it easily becomes a downward spiral, which goes hand in hand with alcohol, drugs and all kinds of destructive behavior. All for not having had a source of love, something that could had helped us to not give up! Many times, all we need, is someone who can be there for us to listen and tell us, that "everything is going to be fine", and that it is "possible to change and be forgiven!", I needed it, but there were times when the only thing that came from other people were words that made me feel how bad I was, and that this world would be a better place without me. Let's be gentle with others, a word of love illuminates, especially the more darkness a person is going through!

Let's start to really heal, and love ourselves to be well, see well and love well. First, we have to be aware if there is something going on, that is robing us from our happiness, we don't have to shout it out to the world, this is between us and God, we just have to acknowledge if something is not right and if we are in need of help! Only by accepting help, we will be open to look for a solution!

It is important to internalize and think about: where the moment was when: "I stopped loving myself and started looking on the outside for what I have to be looking within me"

What happened? What made me change my essence?

The Light That I Carry in Me

I know there are very difficult times, but you are not alone, and it is worth fighting, for you. You are worth it, please don't give up. I wanted to give up so many times! Now I thank from the bottom of my heart; that I didn't do it! But I also give thanks to God for being there, helping me through other people in all the difficult times! Now I'm at peace, I know that many things had to happen, others could have been avoided!
But in the same way, I wonder:
Why this happened to me?
What was the cause?
What do I have to learn from all this?

I understand: I am the man, I am! Thanks to all the things I went through, I will not use nothing as an excuse, nor will I start victimizing myself saying: why me?
And who else?

It happened to me and "that's it" I decided today to let go! Of everything that prevents me, from loving myself as I am. It's just a decision, I decide to focus on loving myself and thanking myself that despite everything, I am still standing and hungrier for life.

There will be nothing and no one to stop me from becoming the best version of myself.
I will fight day after day, minute after minute, against the only person who can take away my happiness: "Myself." Nobody else, just me against me.

I will put myself first, I will take myself into account, enough of putting myself last, I am a child of God too and I deserve a new opportunity, I want it and I claim it, and I will take advantage of

Fireproof Knights

it!

If you did something bad and you think that you do not deserve love, you are completely wrong! YES, you do DESERVE IT! And by being well, full of healthy love, you will be able to help much more, perhaps the damage you caused was too much, but try to give back as much as you can while you have a breath of life, contribute everything you can. If you are really sorry; Bear fruits of repentance and bless God for giving you a new opportunity. Not all of us have it, others left without having the opportunity to make up for their faults.

Remember, this is a path for brave people, warriors who no longer use any excuse to become the best version of themselves. Warriors who recognize that, even if they do not always feel it, even if they are full of doubts and fear, they will walk with fear hand in hand and overcome it day by day. Warriors who know what is right and necessary, who are part of the change by decision, not by obligation, or by threat.

Repeat constantly:
"I love myself and I am worthy of a new opportunity, what I was, I let go! What happened to me, I let it go! What I did, I let it go at this moment! Out of love and mercy, I declare myself free from any bondage that prevents me from loving."

I know that showing love to others and to ourselves is something that we do not know how to do, because we were not taught! We do not know how to distinguish it, because possibly we have never really felt it. We may be confused thinking what it is, but perhaps it is not even close. Real love, it is felt, does not require saying it, it does not require being shouted at so that others find out, it is a circle of trust, between those who are part of it.

The Light That I Carry in Me

Think about the love of God, I share with you what I feel:

The love of my Father God is so beautiful, I feel free and completely accepted, there are no judgments, there are no condemnations, it is so great and so intense that it goes through every cell of my body and restores my being, Father God gives me and asks nothing of me. In return for Him, what He asks is for me, it will serve me and it is for my own well-being, I do not need to explain to anyone, nor ask for any opinion, or wait for someone's approval. It's between Him and Me.

If you have something beautiful, where you don't have to say I LOVE YOU, it is felt, expressed in many ways: Through physical contact, a kiss, a hug; by sharing time together, through gifts, by preparing food, or taking care of the other person when they are sick, by providing, or taking care of what they have together, and with words that can range from: How was your day? Have you eaten yet? Need help?

Without knowing it, we have been surrounded by love everywhere and at all times. It's just that we all express it in different ways, maybe we are not used to saying I LOVE YOU, but we use all love languages continuously with all the people around us. We just need to be conscious, and put more intention and meaning into it and we will see the magic of love.

Love is around us, all the time. The secret is to imitate nature. Have you ever wondered if the sun ever asks for something in return? Or the moon? "They only give", in the same way we, from now on, give love to each person, let your energy and your good intentions towards everyone be felt, through your words, interactions, looks, gestures and little by little you will see how everyone around you begins to naturally return what you have planted.

Now, just take care of your mind and don't let anything or anyone get involved in it, with thoughts different from what you want for your life, because love must be pure, without malice or bad intentions, so that it produces only good things.
It may take a while for you to adapt to a new way of loving, it doesn't matter, step by step is fine, it's worth the effort, to reach the moment when you feel in harmony with the world. All beings that vibrate at that new frequency will become more and more. And little by little with correct love, we will transform our environment to give faith and witness to what we carry inside.

Love yourself, take care of yourself and seek your happiness, enjoy life.

God bless you and; HÉ may fill your heart with self-love and passion for living.

The Light That I Carry in Me

CHAPTER 19

❧

It's Okay to Say "No"

For a long time, I felt bad or guilty when someone asked me for money and I said NO, because I thought that as a Christian it was up to me, to say yes to everyone who asked for help. Then when I lent "x" amount of money, time passed and I never saw it again, nor the person, much less what was lent. The problem is not helping, simply the amount we give, it has to be an amount that we are willing to part with, think of it as donating money, if it comes back, it will be very well received and if not, we had already given that money away before. But by giving it from the beginning, somewhat unwillingly, from that moment, from "the doubt" it is possible that the amount will not be seen anywhere again, and what will replace it is the feeling of regret, the sensation of having Being stupid, to trust and lend so easily, a feeling of lack arises in one and something that could have been something positive for everyone, something that would have meant a pact or an alliance, creates a trapped negative energy. And now every time that person comes to mind, it will be accompanied by many negative thoughts. Someone once told me, "Do you want a person to disappear from your life? Lend him money!"

Saying NO would have been the best option.

Don't complicate your life, it's okay to say NO, if you can't, you can't.

Fireproof Knights

In the beginning, it is okay to help in many other ways, especially when you are starting to live, without involving money. How are you going to give something you don't have, and how are you going to have more, if you don't learn to say NO. Managing your resources will take you far in life.

Vitamin N is one of the best vitamins that you can take daily and constantly, because all the time we are pressured to say Yes, to countless activities, people, or situations that only steal our time, our energy and money; which in turn is time, which costs us to earn.

We all have a certain amount of energy each day, energy that is up to us to manage, and if we are constantly sabotaging ourselves by saying yes to things we don't want, then it will be difficult for us to have the energy needed for the things that really matter.

Also get used to depending on yourself and avoid putting someone in the same situation. If you ask, be aware of the effort of the person who is helping you. Have your word and comply with what was agreed, if you ask for a loan, return it in spades! And always value the person who helped you. But remember that you opened the door to also do the same for that person in the future.

Don't make it a habit to ask only thinking about your well-being, always think about how everyone can win. So, every time you ask for help or give help, it becomes an opportunity to create ties, build bridges of opportunity, and unite alliances.

Before saying yes to something that you are not completely sure about, take some time before answering, usually, we all have a moment when we are excited, and whether it is because of the environment, the atmosphere, the emotion of the moment, or because pressure; We are easy prey for many people, and it's not that it's wrong or right, sometimes we need all these circumstances and that pressure, which is absolutely necessary to get out of our comfort zone, but the point is, we have to have the Sufficient control to be able to say NO, without guilt, without regrets, without complexes, or dilemmas.

It's okay to wait, take things slowly. Remember that a NO, is not permanent, maybe it is the right person, it is the right thing, it is what vibrates to you, it is what you want, it is everything but the time; It's not the right one! If you put things forward, you put the result at risk and in the end, you will have wanted to wait.

Accept a NO, in the same way, learn to take a NO, and do not take it personally, there are many reasons why you can receive a NO, and usually it always has to do with the other person, or the time, not with you. The more you remember that a NO is also a positive thing, the more you will understand the power and blessing it brings.

When you receive a negative result, especially regarding your health, do not rush to accept that illness, or condition that forces you to live in a different way, with fear, sadness or anguish. Especially if it is followed by an amount of time that limits you to being here in this world. Question it, entrust yourself to God and say:

"NO, in the name of God, I reject it."

"Never accept something you don't want, no matter who tells you" If you feel your health is really affected, you can consciously work on it and improve, change your habits and regain your health, "Remember everything is possible for him who believes."

There are many times that we decide to act where we have not even been asked to do so, we say yes out of love, but many times a NO is necessary and can be out of love too. There are beings that we love, who are in bad steps, trapped in addictions and conflicts where they do not see clearly, therefore, whatever we do will go unnoticed, a NO can be the solution that leads them to hit rock bottom and react! Accepting help is difficult and each situation requires deep thought, but a NO is also valid, because it is our life that is affected too, and sometimes we do more by doing nothing!

Remember that we live in a world where the degree of unconsciousness is still very great, and many of the things we do or commit to do, we do without thinking, for instance:

When I was around 15 years old, I went to a friend's house that I loved very much, and I did my best to go see her frequently, because I liked her a lot. We used to talk outside her house, but at the entrance to her neighborhood, would meet many gang members, one of them always said hi tom me, I even thought we were friends, I didn't know what they did at the entrance to the neighborhood, but I never paid any attention to it. According to me, they only met to talk, "just like I did with my friends." Until one day this boy approached me and with a friendly voice said: I want you to do me a favor! I hadn't finished saying yes, when he pulled out a knife, I don't know from where, and gave it to me, will you keep it for me? He asked, and well I didn't say no! and I didn't even ask why? I remember we only walked about a block and he asked me to give it back, and it was easy for me to return the knife, when out of nowhere, he tried to stabbed me with the

The Light That I Carry in Me

same knife, by a miracle I managed to grab his upper arm and the tip of the knife only grazed my stomach. I felt really scared, but I gathered courage and told him to stop. He replied: "I already found out that you are from another neighborhood, and I am going to kill you for that", I got angry and yelled at him: "You are crazy! Let go!"

Just then some people were coming, so he let me go and left. I trembled away from that place, I never told anyone in my house, I knew that my mother would not let me go outside the house, if she had found out. Now I reflect that, it can even cost us our lives rushing to say yes. I know that sometimes the pressure that other people put on us, can be a lot, but if it's worth it, can wait! To say NO, is something that is necessary and indispensable.

There are people who ask for money with the intention to not pay it back, we have to be aware if we are being used, for what we can give! I am not against giving but we have to be clear if we are respected and in control!

It is important to know: how much? How? To whom? Why? For what? Your money and your help will be used? We all have resources that could serve a person who really needs it, but many times we use them on people who neither need them nor take advantage of them, nor appreciate them.

When there are doubts about something, we can always ask God for help to find the truth, that is one of the qualities of God, "The Truth." Ask for the truth to manifest and wait, that the answer will soon come.

Take care of your body, you don't have to give yourself, or to say YES to anything, that you don't want, it belongs only to you,

Fireproof Knights

and any decision you make with it will accompany you; for the rest of your life. There are decisions that are not easy to make, perhaps you need to wait until you have a greater degree of maturity, and more clarity in what you decide to do, never believe that something is right or not, due to the number of people for or against it. Decide with your heart, and consciously ask! Inform yourself and analyze every angle! So that later you do not regret it and carry guilt that could have been avoided. There are decisions that are irreversible and that can mark your life in a very negative way! Is better to inform ourselves well, before an important decision, not to take it too lightly, to ask people who are in the same situation, and also those who were in that dilemma a long time ago, would they make the same decision again? Or
would they change their decision?
Is there a better solution?
Is this what I really want to do?
It's my decision?
Am I being suggested by someone or something?
How will my life change with this decision?

There are many questions to answer, always before an important decision, better decide calmly, and be confident with the answer!
And always remember:

There is more time than life *So, let's make better decisions to get the best out of our life!*

The Light That I Carry in Me

CHAPTER 20

⚜

The Power of Words

In a forest 2 little frogs were jumping, from one moment to the next without realizing how, both fell into a hole too deep to escape, but by a miracle they managed to support themselves on a small piece of rock, which served as a springboard every time they descended, they could not rest, there was no space to be supported, the only thing they could do was jump! And when they fell, lean on that little piece of rock to jump again! And when they jumped, they were still very far from being able to escape, doing so would be a practically impossible task, but in the same way they kept jumping; trying to get out.

Many other little frogs who saw what happened came forward to help, but when they saw how deep the hole was, they felt that the effort was no longer worth it, they felt sorry for the situation of the trapped little frogs and instead tried to stop that suffering in vain, because they believed that there was no more hope, that it was best for them to let themselves die, so they used their voices to shout at them: stop! Don't jump anymore! There's no point! Let yourselves fall better! Don't be stupid! Then one of the little frogs gave up and began to jump less and less until it let itself die; by falling into the depths of that hole. On the other hand, the other little frog jumped with more and more force, until it achieved the impossible for everyone! It came out and when the other little frogs approached
To ask why she didn't give up his attempt, they realized that the little frog couldn't hear! The whole time she thought they were

encouraging her to get out.

This is how with our words we can sink a person who is in a hole, or we can motivate them with words to achieve the impossible.

Each word has an amazing power, a vibration and it is with our words that we enchant everything around us, the word when it is released has a specific purpose to fulfill. Whether it is building or destroying, and generally we all take this privilege so lightly, that we sow seeds of everything wherever we want, less than what should be sown. We condemn a person for the mistake committed.

We charm our children with phrases that have a strong emotional impact on their lives, and for us it was a simple call of attention. We hurt their feelings, we mark them, and we constantly clip their wings. With all kinds of phrases that we say just to say. Since they were little, we have called them by nicknames that we find cute, such as: chubby, short, skinny, dummy etc. It's sad how we use our voice to bring down a person, and for us nothing is more fun than telling the current gossip.

We offend and curse the days, saying:
The day is going to be bad because it is raining! It's too hot, we're not going to sell!
Hey, today I woke up on the wrong foot!
Oh, today is Monday, how bad, the same thing again! It's Friday, the week is almost over, how good!

We do not know what we say, but it is time to pay attention to what we say, it is time to create awareness of our words and remember all the time that with them we are building our future,

The Light That I Carry in Me

and that of the people around us, especially when We are in charge of our children's future.

We have to be very clear about this, because they are easily suggestible by us, seeing us as their superheroes, they will believe everything we tell them! Specially in those first years, then our presence and advice will influence almost the rest of their lives. If I ask you something in this book and I want you to take it as a special favor to me! It is that: you no longer speak unkindly, in a harsh and inappropriate way, please no longer yell at them! I understand that being parents is very complicated! Even more, when we do not know what we do and when we are unhappy! Let's not take it out on them!

Let's give them the opportunity that we didn't have, not by giving material things, but rather, helping them to raise awareness from a young age, let's give them the knowledge so that they can make the best decisions, let's explain to them, like the mini adults that they are, the consequences of doing the wrong things. Let them learn wisdom in other mirrors, let us teach them that, they do not have to go through any problems to learn, nor have to suffer so much in life, lets teach them to love themselves for who they are! To say sorry when they make mistakes; to forgive themselves and to not carry grudges with no one, and that they are capable of achieving anything they set their mind to! To feel proud of who they are and their roots, let them know; to seek their happiness! To feel gratitude and express it with intention, and let them know that God loves them above all

It is up to us to sow a new generation that bears fruits of love,

Fireproof Knights

peace, life, intelligence, prosperity, abundance, compassion. It is up to us to allow the bad to last or to find its end.

Let's start with ourselves, let's change the conversations we tell ourselves, let there be love and compassion and all kinds of beautiful words that make us feel important and worthy, because we are!

Let's use the mirror and look into each other's eyes; Let's give an I LOVE YOU, a THANK YOU FOR EVERYTHING, a WE'RE GOING TO BE WELL, and I FORGIVE YOU AND ACCEPT YOU, as YOU COUNT ON ME, and I AM PROUD OF YOU.

And with our words we can begin to make a difference. Let's build a different world around us. Let us always keep in mind words that motivate others. And that they make us believe in being better. And little by little, everything around us will transform; because we transform! Everything changes when we change! Everything improves when we improve! It is on us! Blessings, wealth, health, abundance, love, prosperity, peace, joy, happiness, great relationships, all is to our reach, we just have to **speak it into existence!**

The Light That I Carry in Me

CHAPTER 21

⚜

Only One Time Exists

The only time that matters and where we can truly have an effect on our lives is now. I want you to relive a memory from the past, ready!

Now I want you to dream with your eyes closed, how do you see yourself in 7 years?

You have both answers, perfect.

Now I want you to answer me: in what time did you live, your past and your future?

Exactly! "In the present", everything converges only in one time, to return to the past, you have to bring a memory hidden in it, and relive it in your mind at this moment, in the same way, the future can only be reached from the now.

This is why the past is like a library that you have to organize in a way that works for you and not against you. Select everything that is extra and simply let it go, ignore it! And the mind alone will realize that, that memory does not deserve to be there, and will no longer be there! If you have sad memories that marked your life, do not relieve them from the feeling! Relive it, more like a spectator watching a movie in a cinema. Those memories are there because they have a specific purpose in your life, create vulnerability and make you appreciate moments of happiness more.

The memories of violence and any trauma are memories that we would like to forget, but they are present because we need to heal them first and in some way work on the experience, to learn from it, although we have no fault in what happened, it is important to position ourselves as simple spectators. In all these processes so as not to include feelings that make you lean towards some specific emotion that prevents us from seeing what we have to see.

"Go into your room and close the door, pray to your father who is in secret and your father who sees in secret will reward you in public"

Your room is you! It is your interior. Your memories, your feelings, your desires, everything is there, with the door closed praying to your father. To truly pray you do it from the present and it is completely crucial that you close the door to any interference or distraction that prevents a connection between you and THE FATHER.

When you pray, you are reliving in the present, what you have been carrying and what you ask to be given to you, that is the future. You are uniting the past, present and future in the same line, for prayer to have power there must be harmony and peace between the 3 times.

"Where two or three are gathered in my name, there I will be," everything is harmony, for there to be a state of fluidity in your life, you cannot be fighting with the past or anxious about the future. Let go of everything that makes you feel bad and focus on living only in the now. Remember that the now is called the present, it is a gift that you have to take advantage of, the more

The Light That I Carry in Me

you focus on each moment of your life, you will realize that there is so much to be thankful for!

When we pray, we open the doors to blessing, if we want to know the answer to our prayers, it is time to meditate! When we meditate; We are in a moment that expands the now and accentuates it, having the possibility of connecting with the source, in a way so deep and unlimited that it moves away from reason and has nuances of enlightenment, where we can find ourselves in a state of peace, w h e r e nothing else matter, feeling is everything, appreciating the moment is the only thing that matters, where a moment in the presence of God is a privilege that we take for granted. And it is in those moments when we feel that the answers are coming, suddenly we know and understand! We see with different eyes, what before was not even important; now has a deeper and more important meaning, with certainty all is possible when we manage to let go of all the noise in our mind interfering with our life and be completely immerse in the presence of the source of life, the consciousness of which we are all part, like drops of the sea in an infinite ocean.

Reconnect with our essence, by having a moment of total presence, without mind, without any thought, perhaps we can be able to see inside long enough to contemplate enlightenment, even for a moment; we can realize that suddenly everything takes on a different shine, the colors look brighter and more alive, the senses of our body become more acute and we can really feel, nothing else is important, the world stops and it is as if the water of a waterfall stops in mid-fall, and it even tries to turn back, it is a magical time, an eternal time, a mystical now, but possible, and in its stillness the beauty of living arises.

Fireproof Knights

Do we understand why the Now is important? Live it, respect it, be grateful for it, and love it, because it is a **privilege**, it is a *gift*, it is a **present!**

The Light That I Carry in Me

CHAPTER 22

❧

Attitude

One of the most important words that you will find in life is "*attitude*" because it is with it that we place ourselves in front of possibilities of success, or with our attitude we close the doors to it, and to endless experiences, and we have to always remember that the only thing we are going to take with us when we leave this world are all the experiences we have lived; But what good is it to remember something that we didn't care about, or where we didn't put interest, passion or enthusiasm?

The attitude towards everything we do, opens the doors of happiness, or catapults us into mediocrity, because if we are not convinced to truly go after everything we love, we are half-believing; And logically we will obtain bad results in everything, we will obtain experiences that will be uninteresting and we will surround ourselves with people who will be on the same frequency, all this because we have a bad attitude towards life.

We have to remember that we can be taught everything, people can be patient with us, we can be working for the first time or starting a romantic, professional or personal relationship, and the only thing that will help us to move forward so we can keep the doors open to achieve our purpose, our objective! Is our ATTITUDE. Someone with a terrible attitude at the beginning has already closed the doors, for me personally it is the only thing that discourages me from wanting to teach, that is *why, we are told that; When the student is ready, the teacher appears! Because "there is nothing more frustrating, than teaching someone who doesn't have the desire to learn", and what does it look like when we don't have the desire?* **Because of the attitude.**

Why not start seeing things with different eyes, expecting to find interesting things to discover, beautiful people to meet, new skills to learn, new books to read. Every day is an opportunity to grow and do what we love most, every second counts, every moment contains the opportunity for a miracle, for something that impresses us and leaves us with a sigh of happiness. Let's be passionate about living with the best possible attitude: optimistic and positive, soon we will see how the mountains move away before our eyes, we will see the hand of God move before us and we will see how all the people treat us in a better way, they smile at us with pleasure and sincerity , opportunities present themselves to us on their own, and love becomes part of our life, that same positive attitude will take us to places we never thought possible to know, it is incredible what an attitude of interest can find in its path.

Let us also recognize, that we may be being driven by a manipulative attitude, or we ourselves may be using this attitude in order to make things work according to the expectations and desires of our mind, using others as objects in order to convince them, through strategies to make them feel that they are the ones who are deciding to do something, when it was the other's idea from the beginning, even if the person manipulating does it with the best of intentions.

The Light That I Carry in Me

What comes hand in hand with this manipulative attitude is the submissive attitude, and it is recognized because people put themselves as objects, to be used either consciously or unconsciously, and people choose to behave this way due to an ancient survival mechanism where they feel protected by the person who manipulates, they feel safe in some way, as they are not the ones carrying the pressure of a decision or responsibility.

A neutral attitude will bring good moments and bad moments, the interest will be half-hearted therefore we will live a half-life, I personally hope, deserve and want the best in life, so I decide to do my best to consciously have the best possible attitude, facing everything in life, always hoping for the best.

There are those who have a flexible attitude towards everything, which allows them to adapt better to all types of situations and people, but always maintaining their identity. On the contrary, there are people who act in an inflexible way, which leads them to disagree with people and circumstances, keeping them in small conflicts, which can lead them to suffer and not allow themselves to fully enjoy where they are.

We can also find people who act in a way that makes us feel judged for our actions, and who at the same time punish themselves in this way, and all because of the system of beliefs they have pre-established with respect to ethics and morals, if something falls outside that parameter, it is wrong and deserves punishment.

Although our attitude is determined by the experiences, actions and emotions that we have lived in the past, at the end of all it is we who decide to react in a different way, one that is more in tune with the type of person in which we desire and we hope to become.

Fireproof Knights

I know that many times it is very difficult to change what is happening in our lives, and much more difficult to distance ourselves from people, with attitudes that are terrible, attitudes so negative that, when being in their presence, we feel like they steal our energy, these are energy vampires!

It is very complicated when we are around people who drain our energy, but in the extent that we choose to react in a different way, a better way, and we do not put our focus on them, only on our attitude, we will be vibrating in a different frequency, so that; These people will change! Or move away! Because we radiate something very different and they simply cannot understand us, much less feel comfortable sharing the same space.

The focus on our attitude makes us realize; If we are really acting the way we should, or if we are doing it automatically, due to the programming we have; If so, it requires total concentration to be aware of ourselves, and surprise ourselves in the act, to consciously replace one attitude with another that contributes to our life, and that allows us to have a certain control to what we expect from it. With just this radical change, we open the doors to a series of possibilities that give us better results.

We can realize, everything is on us, and to the extent that we have a conscious mentality of our attitude at all times, we will have taken a gigantic step towards a better life.

The Light That I Carry in Me

CHAPTER 23

⚜

A Three Part Story
First part

Some time ago, I found myself alone, between the sand and the foam of the sea, with my gaze lost on the horizon, with tears in my eyes because of the pain, and the feeling of helplessness that I felt when punishing myself, with the memory of a relationship that it shouldn't have been, I felt empty and the alcohol in me! Did not alleviate my feelings, but it made me feel brave in the face of the power of the sea. I remember: when I entered it, and as I was dodging waves, there was a moment of stupidity on my part, where with a defiant tone; I said "this is all you have."

But I didn't know that, from one moment to the next, everything would change, that calm and serene ocean; went from that to, sending waves that exceeded my height by far and when I wanted to swim out, I felt like a current below my waist was dragging me. With force, I sank for a few seconds and when I came out, I saw the sky completely cloudy and gray, I was deep in the sea, I kept on moving my hands and feet, to avoid sinking, I didn't know where the dizziness from the alcohol went, I just knew that every 6 or 7 seconds a new wave formed and I had to sink a little to avoid it, I tried to swim out, but I didn't make any progress, in the distance I could see
the shore, and I tried to scream and make gestures with my hands, but it was useless, no one seemed to notice my agony. The moment came when I couldn't take it anymore, after many

Fireproof Knights

minutes of fighting for my life, my entire body began to fail me, I didn't know what to do, I was afraid! I was scared and my mind already began to contemplate the idea of my death. At that moment, I could only think about my mother and my brothers, and how I couldn't say goodbye to them, I didn't want to die!, but at the same time, I began to think that it was time to get right with God, before I was not longer conscious, and it was too late to ask for forgiveness, rather than feeling guilty about something, I felt disappointed, because I felt that I had wasted my life, and that at my young age, I wasted my time! I remember, I looked at the sky and said to Father God "Thank you" and "sorry".

I let myself be defeated, my body stopped fighting, I gave up, my mind went blank, there were no thoughts, there was nothing, my heart seemed to be the only one that still clung to life, little by little I began to swallow water, and I felt death for a couple of seconds, and how it took hold of me; by depriving me of oxygen.

I don't know where I got the strength from, but there was only one word in my mind at that last moment, "I can't die like this." I began to kick and use my arms to stay afloat, I regained my strength and for a moment I could see towards the shore, but my eyes crossed with an angel, someone was swimming towards me, and in an instant, he was pulling me out, in less than within 20 seconds we were outside, I still couldn't believe what had happened to me. One of my best friends approached me and told me "I was drowning too," but they managed to get me out.
And I told them that you were still inside, and they went for you", I thanked everyone for saving my life! I looked up at the sky and smiled, I turned my gaze to the sea and looked at it with respect from that day on.

The Light That I Carry in Me

Fireproof Knights

Second Part

Less than a year ago, my kind friend, who was the one who invited me to meditate for the first time, approached me and after greeting me with love and with that wonderful heart that she has, she told me: I had a dream about you, it was so real. And I know that sooner or later you will understand it, she told me:

In my dream there were many people near to the sea, all of them in white clothes, their eyes full of illusion, hope in their faces, I was closer to the sea and suddenly I saw how a figure came out of it; figure like a man, but his entire body was made of sea water. In my heart I felt, that it was God walking towards me, in the middle of his hands he carried a pearl, as beautiful as unique, God gave it to me, and gave me precise instructions to be delivered to you. "That you would understand." And that's where my dream ended, she said.

My friend said goodbye to me with a big hug, and with a look of deep respect, admiration and love for each other. I spent a lot of time thinking about the meaning of that dream, which my friend shared, but no matter how hard I tried, the answer didn't come.

The Light That I Carry in Me

Third Part

And the answer eluded me! I felt as if God, wanted to tell me something but at the same time, God wanted me to work to find out. The days went by and nothing, until one afternoon, almost at night, I was able to connect with God through meditation. I began the breathing process required to reach a deeper level of tranquility where gradually, I was able to connect to the source. "When I am in that state everything flows in a different way for me, it is as if I have access to all the information I need"

One of the responses that changed and that marked a before and after in understanding how God sees me. Was the answer to my friend's dream, that same answer that I was seeking to find out, since that conversation; It came to me like a ray of light that illuminated me and everything made sense.

"You are the pearl that I took from the sea"

For a long time, I had forgotten that; I still had the breath of life, thanks to the fact that I was rescued from the sea, thanks to God who did not allow me to drown, it was thanks to God that help came that day, thanks to Him I still I had an opportunity to do everything I loved, it was incredible that I had forgotten that moment, but it was like that, I was too young to understand, I was too immature to recognize that it was God, through someone else, who took me out of the sea. I had never been told something so beautiful, and that contained so much in a single sentence, how special I am to God, and the way He compares me to a pearl! Not only because of the beauty of the jewel, also because the pearl; It

Fireproof Knights

has its origin from a Persian word "Murwari" that means: "daughter of light" a symbol of purity, faith and hope for me.

By understanding that he pulled me out of the sea, I recognize that my life has a special meaning, that I was given a new opportunity, and that from that precise moment, I was allowed to live, to do what I really love, for when I have to say goodbye one day , to be certain that on that time: I did take advantage of my time, that I did everything that filled me with happiness, that I truly loved, that I made a difference in the lives of the people who were by my side, that every day, I overcame any given obstacle that could have prevented me from achieving my dreams and goals, now I understand that it is only about working on myself, and that it is in myself, the possibility of having a life that is worthy of being remembered.

And one of those dreams, for me, was always the idea of writing a book; Today, thank God, you are part of that vision that becomes a reality. To write a book, with the intention of being able to share it with who thirsts, for a better world. By writing it, I realized that I found a deeper way to remember, to put my thoughts in order, to have the opportunity to talk about my experiences, to provide a ray of light to a confused and unconscious mind through the written word. I found the possibility of being able to advise and have a conversation with my children forever, who, although I cannot physically be present, will carry in this book the best of me, the essence of who I am. I hope in God, to have the possibility of continuing living, in my being I have the illusion of doing many more things, but I decide to live from now, one day at a time, plan for tomorrow, but nothing more than a point of reference, my life belongs to God, and by my decision I sail with him as the captain of my ship, without fear, because God is in control of everything, but with the

The Light That I Carry in Me

illusion of what can be and with **the faith, that it will be so.**

Fireproof Knights

The Light That I Carry in Me

CHAPTER 24

⚜

With The Fear in Hand

Fear can be a very important teacher if we learn to see it for what it really is. For thousands of years, human beings have faced all kinds of dangers, the earth was a hostile and dangerous place, where life could be lost at any time, for any reason. It was very important to be aware of our surroundings at all times.

Fear was necessary, it was fear that kept us cautious of the unknown, and it was that necessary brake, which prevented us from trusting ourselves in any situation, where our life could be in danger. That brain, cautious, prehistoric, is still with us and continues to do its job, for which it was wonderfully created; And it is manifested by that fear that paralyzes you when you are experiencing something new, something different from what you are used to. Do not get angry with yourself, for those nerves, for that feeling of paralysis, for that uncontrollable sweating, for that trembling in your body, all these are signals that your brain sends to your body to communicate with you, seeking to make you give up, in your attempt to learn new and different things, unless we are really in a dangerous situation! It is our duty to expose ourselves to what we are afraid of, so our brain understands that there is no real danger, that we are safe and that this is the path we want to go through.

Fireproof Knights

Let the brain know that we will be fine, and everything will be okay on that occasion when we need to speak in public, and express our thoughts. When we are trying to talk to that special person, but we completely freeze when taking the first step. It happened to me, when I was 9 years old and I wanted to ask a 14-year-old girl to dance. I thought about it so much, for many days, I tried and tried, but every time I had a small opportunity to talk to her, I was paralyzed and couldn't find the words, until one day I grabbed fear by the hand, and asked her: would you like to go to the school dance with me? She just smiled at me and said: "you are so sweet, but I'm sorry I have a boyfriend."

In part I already expected that answer, but I felt proud that I had the courage to face fear and finally defeat it. Without knowing it, this is where I began to challenge one of the best teachers I have ever had.

Fear is that feeling in our stomach, moments before being in a situation that takes us out of our comfort zone, but exactly, at that moment when it becomes present, at that precise moment when we realize what we are going to do. Is that the time to face our limit, and that's how we have the opportunity to overcome it, and prepare for a new challenge.
Fear disappears once we face it, when we expose ourselves to what we are afraid of, it gives up and calms down because our mind let it know that there is no real danger. For a long time, I had a fear of expressing myself in front of many people, even with one person it was already difficult to me. I felt that my legs were shaking just for the thought of doing it, if I had to give a presentation in front of the class, all kinds of thoughts came that fueled that fear, and it was the worst experience ever.

The Light That I Carry in Me

It was horrible, until I had the opportunity to face it as an adult, with total control of my senses, I was able to move forward, and it was at that moment that I "continued to be afraid", but fear would no longer paralyze me, I made the conscious decision from that day that every time I felt afraid, I would take it as a sign of growth, and that the reward would come into my life after that act of courage.

Many times, the fear is due to past traumas, I had a very serious problem communicating and expressing my feelings, I even had problems with my speech, I stuttered in moments of tension.

It was after a meditation, that I had a regression in my mind, and I went back to the age of 6 years old, when my mother without any bad intentions, had put me in the white pajamas with pink stripes that belonged to my sister, and modified them so that I looked like a little fox, for a school play. I remember as soon as I entered school, all the children pointed at me and made fun of me. Finally, they took me to the stage, in front of the entire school; I had to say my line: I paused, I knew what I had to say, but I was left speechless when I saw everyone's expression and laughter. Finally, I said "the sky is falling" and I stepped back, from that day on, I was never the same. I had that memory saved in my unconscious, and I was able to heal it by facing it again; And that speech and communication problem completely disappeared. Now I even dare to sing karaoke, can you imagine!

It's amazing what bravery can do with our lives. When you have a situation to face, just be brave for 20 seconds, don't think about it, just do what you have to do, and after those seconds your brain will realize that there is no danger and will stop its efforts to make you feel afraid. And if you still feel it, it will be to a lesser extent, controllable.

"Be strong and
 courageous,
  the Lord tells us."

The Light That I Carry in Me

CHAPTER 25

⚜

Our Enemy

The battle takes place in the least expected place, within our mind. This is the field where day by day we advance or retreat, from where we can conquer or leave defeated.

The enemy is not outside, he is on the inside, and it is our mission not to allow him to take over us. It is very subtle and cunning; it generates dramas and all kinds of conflicts to divert our attention from what is truly important: Becoming our best version! It constantly confuses us by sowing all kinds of tares.

Our ego is responsible for so much suffering, so much conflict and so many lost opportunities, it makes us believe that we are fine, and that the problem is other people. And this is how we all attack each other, seeing the bad in others and never in ourselves, when in reality others are mirrors of ourselves, showing us what we must work on in ourselves. It is said that, if something bothers you in someone, pay attention to it, it is more than certain that you have the same problem to solve, when you admire something about someone, you recognize a quality in yourself and this makes you feel very good when in the presence of said person, bending our knees is the best way to keep the ego away from controlling us! The ego cannot bear to feel that it is in such a noble position, because it is haughty and proud, and its *vanity is incapable of, "according to it", being reduced to less. And it's not that God needs us to worship him in that way, what we achieve is to quiet, any internal voice that prevents us from being in true communion with God. It is necessary to put ourselves in a state of learning, and humbly receive some message, some advice or simply to be in a more favorable position to accept being corrected.*

The ego always seeks to be right in everything. And sticks to it, it doesn't care about doing the most unpleasant and unthinkable thing and coming out as the winner. On the contrary, our true nature, which seeks to always be at peace, seeks to raise the level of consciousness and seeks our happiness, is not interested in seeing who is right. Our true nature just flows, lives, learn, grows, adapts, modifies itself, is reborn, and continues. Always existing in a continuous state of transformation.

The ego reduces us to simple mortals, when in reality what we are goes far beyond any deception or mirage, we are much more than, we can imagine! We have only forgotten it, but it is time for us to begin to believe and give ourselves the opportunity to rise as champions!

The ego makes us believe that we have to prove that we are the best to be valuable as a person, it keeps us in a constant war, which does not let us experience the beauty of living, we keep fighting with the people around us for not reason. We don't have to prove absolutely anything! we are better off just with knowing that we are children of God! And the only thing we have to be interested in is: searching and doing what makes us happy.

The more the ego controls us, the more distant we are from

The Light That I Carry in Me

reality, the less it controls us, the closer we are to the truth and what is important! Of course, there are many differences in the degree of control from one person to the next.

The good thing is that, our feelings are the thermostat that tells us; whether our way of acting is correct or not, and by nature try to bring us to a state of balance, and that is where the internal conflict is created, between what we must do and all kinds of thoughts that tell us:
don't lower yourself!
You are too much to admit, that you were wrong!
Let the other person apologize!
Why do you?

And this battle can last a lifetime, there are even people who carry anger since they were young and who remember as if it were yesterday, 60 years later, anger over things as trivial as not having been invited to a wedding, or for not having been greeted in the correct way. Ego tells us: Don't change anything!

The first thing, to find a solution to something, is to recognize that there is a problem, even if it is small. The sooner we realize that all we have to do, is recognize that the ego exists in us. It exists in everyone! It is like our shadow, the lighter we shine, the more possibilities it has to grow. Have you seen how the shadow is capable of creating all kinds of shapes and figures when is generated by light? Likewise, the ego creates all kinds of illusions and mirages to control our mind and our feelings. See how it controls us?
And acknowledge, how it activates?
What makes it react and detonate?
Study it well, to find all kinds of tools to prevent it from getting out of control.

Fireproof Knights

The ego will always exist, it is ready to ruin our life in a minute, the secret is to let go of the confrontation and see it as an ally, every time it is present in us, know the reason for its appearance, and the more we understand it, the more we can use it to our advantage to improve and overcome obstacles.

All of this will lead us to understand that all human beings are fighting a battle with their egos, in addition to all kinds of other battles! Be aware of this so, we can have compassion for others, there are those who are having a rough time!

The important thing now, is to work on ourselves and see how much control the ego has over us. Regaining control of our authentic being, is our main priority! We have to have a point of reference, to know where we are starting from, and after a while understand what we need to work on us, and again, as many times as need it, in our life, and by doing so, will also realize that our quality of life will be better in all aspects, because it is directly related to our ego, the more control over the ego, the better quality of life.

The ego always needs recognition to exist, there are many people who have a wonderful heart, they have done everything well, they have let go of everything that hindered them to be in grace with God, they have dedicated their lives to helping others and they have done it all from the heart, they are full of qualities that make them great leaders, excellent people, and wonderful human beings, but they encounter the last obstacle in their paths:

"The Spiritual Ego"

It is when we forget that everything comes from God and it is

The Light That I Carry in Me

thanks to Him, that we can do what we love, and we are able to help others, all begins when we forget we are only instruments for a cause greater than ourselves, and we are never the ones to be praise, but God!

Sometimes the degree of attachment to those in the service of God, can be so strong that many could get confuse and have a feeling of veneration towards them! The bigger the position we are able to hold, the humbler we have to be, when at the service to others! Because when being at a better position, we can see more clearly and understand the reasons why. Many people cannot get out of where they are, reasons that prevent them from being; what they are destined to be, this gives us a higher perspective, and we cannot feel anything other than deep compassion and gratitude.

What did we do wrong?
Why do we need to prove that we are not bad?
Why do we need to prove that we are the best?
Why do we have to forget about our happiness, to fit in?
Why are we so afraid to let go of ego?
What did we lose by letting ego get in the way?
Isn't our happiness worth more than being right?
Isn't love more than just looking for company?
Isn't peace more than living disturbed by the murmur of meaningless words?
Isn't the life of a being more than having an endless number of soulless things?
Isn't our soul more than anything we might have?
And aren't we worth more, by possessing all the most beautiful things that can exist in us?

Each neuron is like the universe, in each cell is the energy to create life, in our DNA is the entire history of the world from the beginning, in our brain is the most perfect computer ever created; impossible to imitate and connected to a body capable of feeling a whole rainbow of emotions, sensations, textures, colors, aromas, flavors, a body designed to experience life in abundance with total fullness, with deep meaning and capable of create life. There is nothing compared to us, absolutely nothing, and instead of focusing on the fullness of our being, on contemplating our creator's creation! And thanking Him with every atom, with every cell, with every breath of life, we deny His existence, and we give power to everything that does not belong to us, to all that is evil, to all that is perverse, to all that destroys, the sin that dwells in us, and these evil lives in us because we have allowed a place to be, we've just been keeping it alive, because we didn't know that everything bad that lives in us, is like an unwanted guest. How long will be like a plague, taking over a place where is not needed, a place that does not love it, a place that is fed up with his evil, and all the unpleasant that it represents?

"*Ego is going to control us until we allow it*"

Enough of enduring this **abuse!**

The Light That I Carry in Me
CHAPTER 26

❦

Our True Nature

Who are we? We are not our mind, nor the thoughts we carry inside, we are not our name, nor our body, not our nationality, not our way of being, we are not our past, nor our history, we are not what we have, or what we possess, we are not our profession, we are not our talents or skills, we are not our last name, or lineage, we are not our mind, nor all its logic, so: What are we?

We are consciousness, souls, spirit in essence, we are beings of light, designed to do good in everything, because it is the good that makes us feel good, if it were the bad that made us feel good, that would be our nature! But it is not. Thus, every person, no matter how bad they are, and no matter how much evil they do, in a moment of consciousness they will return to their true nature, and realize everything bad they have done, everything! And will feel remorse, even if it is for a moment. We are in a punishing society, and we forgot that these beings who do harm, were once children who came into a world; in which, they were not fortunate enough to have the necessary resources to grow well, they encountered endless problems, traumas, abuses and situations that forced them to be different, they found a world hostile, where they were not accepted for who they are! For this, they are not the bad things they have done! They are the good things they could have done! Perhaps that generation no longer has a solution, because evil is so permeated that its nature refuses to inhabit a world in such a state. As if they knew that death or confinement is better than the possibility of harming

Fireproof Knights

someone else.

I remember when I was younger, I heard a conversation from adults who said that the gang members of that time, before doing harm, made sure that the victims were not Christians or elderly people, much less children; They had a code that they respected and they knew that even evil had a limit and they could not live in peace if they exceeded it.

Doing harm to those who do harm to us, is like an eye for an eye, but with that we give continuity to the evil. That is why our teacher Jesus, came to help us understand a better path, where we work to put an end to evil from the root. If someone hurts , us, we choose to act in a way more in accordance with our nature, with love and compassion, doing good to the person who is doing us wrong, but at the same time; showing that we are not willing to tolerate such treatment, it will be in the person's hands to react, but we have shown the kind of person we are, it is as if we are giving a sample of our being and what we carry inside, when we carry the load for 2 miles, instead of one, as we were forced to: what I see is to show that by being with God, we can do more than a normal person could   endure, we will be giving a huge blown to the ego, whoever wants to take advantage of us, implying that with God by our side there is nothing that can stop us. The important thing is to have character and let it be known that we will not be trampled, that our nature is like water: soft, abundant, calm, refreshing, but at the same time powerful and imposing.
Being good and calm does not make us weak and stupid, it is not about letting someone humiliate us, it is not about letting someone abuse us, it is not about letting injustice prevail, it is not about resigning ourselves to a world where we have no voice, a world where our children do not have a future worth the effort to live.

The Light That I Carry in Me

It's not about fighting, it's about shining brighter and showing everyone who crosses our path the difference in how things should be done, inviting them without words, motivating them with our actions, making them see in us, a source of inspiration, a model to follow. That is why, by expanding our light, we illuminate the lives of everyone around us, and there is no darkness or shadow that can be hidden, they simply cannot stand our shine and end up disappearing. Just remember that real brilliance comes with the absence of ego, otherwise, your brilliance would generate envy and confrontation, every action of us would come with an idea of provocation, it is as if we were saying: "This year, I will be the best version of myself, even if it hurts them." From the beginning we are opening the door to negative energy, we do not need to prove anything, nor say our plans, nor mention how blessed we are! "When we are, we are" we don't need to show off, we simply are and that's it!

The path of a warrior of God, is as easy as letting go, and as difficult as when we hold on to something, with all our strength! It depends solely and exclusively on us, how much we advance, or how much we want to be in the same place, there is no rush, we carry the load, we will know if it weighs enough for a transformation! We impose the rhythm, it is as slow or fast, as we decide! And it will take as long as it takes! Each process is different, every sunrise is wonderful! And it would be a pleasure to witness how the darkness of the night of this humanity gives way, to the morning of the awakening of consciousness that gives us entry to the fifth dimension. A change that we have waited for so long, where courage is required, for things that need to happen, but that are part of a **cycle that must be fulfilled.**

Fireproof Knights
NOTES

The Light That I Carry in Me

CHAPTER 27

❧

Let's Heal the Past

How to start? Is different for everyone, it is more about recognizing where we are and starting from that point, because the healing work is cyclical, meaning that no matter where we start, we will return to the same place, sooner or later we will resume what was previously worked on, but at a deeper level.

By healing the past, we heal the present!

What we have to do next is to go to a previous chapter, and have a second opportunity to work more deeply on what we carry inside, that is affecting us; but this time we will do it with more determination to turn our lives around in the present, and to once and for all, leave behind everything that could hinder us from achieving our dreams! "One situation at a time" we can return to this chapter whenever we decide to do so, each time trying to do so, with more determination.

Just focus on this thought:
"My healing depends on me"

That's all it took to understand, it doesn't depend on anyone else, "it just depends on me."

Fireproof Knights

If you think about it, it is even liberating, you do not depend on anyone else, you do not have to wait, you do not have to put yourself in second place, by being completely focused on yourself and your healing, it will be faster, more effective, more dignified, because even if we have a person who helps us, part of us will never want this person to fully find out the truth, for fear of feeling judged, for shame, because from that moment the perspective that is held of us will change, because only we can understand our truth, many times we do not even find the words to explain what happened; So much so, that something happens to us and for the rest of people, suddenly turns out that we are the ones to be blamed! Has this happened to you? To me, many times!

In this exercise, we will heal episodes from our past, we will change the past and the energy we have trapped in it, and that will make our present feel different.

It consists of traveling to an episode where we feel that in some way it could have been different, either because we didn't like the outcome, or because marked our life in some profound way. We are going to start with something, not that deep or challenging and then as we move forward, we will be able to work on more deeper problems. "We can increase or decrease the degree of seriousness, of that what we want to heal, in harmony with how secure we are feeling with the process"

Healing steps:

It is always important to find a quiet and comfortable spot,

The Light That I Carry in Me

where we can feel secure and have the time to experience healing, reed the steps to know what we need to do ahead of time, and focus deeply on each and every step of the process.

1. With our eyes close relax by taking deep breaths and visualize the memory in vivid detail, see the sights, hear the sounds, let our mind bring it to the present moment as if it were happening again.

2. Now it is very important that we engage our senses, we need to experience the pain, frustration, anger, shame, guilt, we need to focus on what is happening at this precise moment, the touch, smell, feelings, people, what happened?

3. Since we have that emotion! We need to express it intensely, think as it is a gallon of acid that we have to release, toxic acid, that has been making our body sick, that acid can have the following name; hatred, guilt, sadness, indifference, envy, jealousy, bitterness, resentment. Recognize what we are feeling and don't let go, in the case of hate, take a good look at it. It's like a snake is wrapped around our stomach injecting venom. The more we see it, recognize it, and stay in the moment the more we can understand and heal. This emotion was hiding, and feeding on us, and by not expressing it, only became stronger and stronger, emotions like hate need to be expressed, if it is not done in that way, it accumulates and that is when we are completely full of hate, when we explode for any reason, simply we never discharge that substance and it gets to the point, that a drop breaks the camel's back. If that is the emotion we are experiencing, we need to express it, repeat it, mention the person causing it, and say "I hate you, I hate you, I hate you!", until you

feel that it is not necessary to repeat it anymore. If the emotion is guilt, we need to repeat that we are sorry: "I'm sorry, I'm sorry, I'm sorry!", until no longer feels necessary. Same with forgiveness, "forgive me, forgive me, forgive me!", until it doesn't feel necessary, and so, with each of the emotions trapped in each event that we want to heal.

4. *Then we will relive the memory but, we just need to see what happened and experience it in the third person. Think as if we are watching a movie and our focus is now on what's happening, if we do it correctly, we will notice different details, we will realize that many of the things were not as serious as we thought, and we can get to understand different points of view.*

5. *We need to reflect on the memory and ask ourselves, why did this happen to me?*
To what end?
This is very important to not repeat the same pattern in the present. It helps us understand how we got into that problem or situation, and helps us recognize the message, the lesson to be learned, the knowledge necessary to move forward in life. It helps us support others, so that the same thing does not happen to someone else close to us.

6. *Now there is a void left in us, by removing all toxic chemicals from our body, we do not need to be scared if we go to the bathroom and see or feel that something putrid has come out of our body, either from using the bathroom, from vomiting, from sweat, gasses, belching. The step here is: "replace that with a feeling of gratitude, to God, to ourselves, to life or to the people who led us to seek that healing." Remember that fire purifies us,*

The Light That I Carry in Me

and without a doubt we have just gone through hell, which was slowly consuming us day by day.

7. This step is just about to reflecting and smiling, we need to stay in silence for as long as possible, we need to rest, healing is not easy, now we need to recover, drink water, sleep, or anything we are feeling like it for as long as we need to.

Having done this exercise correctly, the result will be an absolute release of that memory, we will be able to remember without feeling a negative emotion, we will see how our health suddenly improves! As we find ourselves with those people who were part of those difficult moments, we will not feel the same as we felt, in fact we might not feel anything, and we will be open to the possibility of feeling compassion for ourselves and for them, empathy and kindness will be present, as well as an endless of positive emotions in all areas of our life.

Suddenly everything looks better and feels better, food suits us well and we enjoy it more. The love we share with our loved ones is more intense and genuine, and above all, we will feel at peace and ready to focus on our dreams and goals.

Fireproof Knights
NOTES

The Light That I Carry in Me

CHAPTER 28

⚜

Pray Without Ceasing

Use affirmations daily of what you want to be manifested in your life. Our brain works like a well-calibrated and sophisticated computer, it also contains many mysteries to reveal, one of those mysteries is "the subconscious"

And one of the qualities that the subconscious has, is to make many of the activities, thoughts, responses, ways of acting, ways of expressing ourselves, behaviors, the way we see life, all of this, done automatically. Without knowing it, during the years that we have been alive, especially the first 7 years, when we are most vulnerable, we have been programming ourselves. The subconscious is in our favor, it acts the way it thinks we want it to.

So, it is up to us to teach ourselves what we really want, what kind of life we want to manifest, and what kind of person we want to be.

And how do we educate it? And how do we sow new programming in it? Something that is more in accordance with a reality that makes us live in peace, happiness, prosperity and full of love? The only way is through constant and conscious *repetition.*

Fireproof Knights

When we don't know something, we are unaware that we didn't know it. "We didn't know the subject." When we know about the subject, we are aware that we know nothing about it! "We decide to learn" now that we know! We are aware that we already know! But we need to be aware all the time to do what we have learned! Now, "since we need to continue learning more and more things" we cannot be conscious all the time in all the activities we do, it would be very exhausting; so, our brain recognizes a pattern in our way of acting based on what we have already learned! It has already studied our way of reacting, of doing things, it knows what we would do in that situation, it decides to make our work easier and sends all this information to the subconscious, with precise instructions on how to do things, the subconscious does not distinguish if it is good or bad, "just obeys."

So, at this point we are unaware that we know, and everything goes on autopilot, our mind is so efficient that it prevents us from spending energy making extra decisions, it decides for us, with the programming that we already have established, in different words on "automatic process"

I don't know about you, but when I was learning to drive, I was aware of everything, that my mirrors, the traffic light, the position of my hands, the position of my feet, my body, the cars, the speed, it was stressful at the beginning. Now there are moments when I just remember getting in the car and getting to my destination, I remember almost nothing of all the little details on my trip, I just arrived. "I Drove on automatic."

Another example is when someone asks us: "How are you?", unconsciously we will always respond in the same way: "Good", unless it is a different day in which something out of the ordinary

The Light That I Carry in Me

happened, we will respond in some other way: "Super good, blessed, bad, very bad, etc."

Remember, everything we repeat constantly will sooner or later manifest in our life, because what we are doing is praying incessantly, "without knowing it", often incorrectly attracting what we don't want. Remember: the subconscious does not know "yes" or "no", it only focuses on the message we focus on and the energy, whether positive or negative, that accompanies it.

So, by understanding this correctly, our mission is to be conscious for a period of 40 days, to change our programming to what we wish to update in our subconscious.

If we always answered: "good", now every time we are asked how are you? We could answer: "Incredibly well, wonderful, super blessed".

And not only we can respond in a better way, but now something more shocking happens, our days begin to unfold the way we change the programming, suddenly our days are as we said they are!

Pray without ceasing, with our eyes closed, open, while we work, while we eat, while we shower, use affirmations that make us feel good, to plant in our subconscious, what we want to see manifested in our life. Pray without ceasing consciously and correctly, using affirmations that make us feel and vibrate in a better way.

I share with you some thoughts that vibrate with me:
Today is a wonderful day.

Fireproof Knights

Today is a blessed day.
God's blessing is with me at all times.
I am happy and prosperous.
I am full of love, health and happiness.
Everything I touch I prosper.
I am always surrounded by wonderful people.
I live heaven here on earth.
I can do all things through Christ, who strengthens me.
I am a child of God, and his blessing is with me.
I let go and trust in God.
I deserve love, peace and happiness.
I am blessed, to bless.
My purpose is to be happy and loved.
I am prosperous and abundant.
Thank you, God, for my good health, for my healthy body, for the beautiful world in which I live.
I praise you Father for my beautiful life and for the opportunity to serve and help my brothers.
I am at peace; I live happy and grateful "Amen".

"So according to my word, and your will beloved Father, be it done."

The Light That I Carry in Me
CHAPTER 29

❦

Always Healthy

It is possible to keep the disease away from our lives for long periods of time. When a person is constantly sick, it is how the body, which is very wise, communicates and is letting us know that there is an emotion that we need to work on and help release, our nature is health in abundance.

The following are examples of people that I love and that I have been able to discern the reason for their symptoms. Each person may present the same symptoms, but the roots of the problem may be different.

When your eyesight fails, it is because of something you are not seeing, something you cling to seeing the way you want it to be and not the way it really is. "That's how clear the body is."

Do you have problems with your breathing? The nose is in front of the body and we do not see it, maybe you have many blessings in life and you are unable to see them? You are so tied to your way of thinking that a blessing, if it is not on your terms is not a blessing.

Do you have problems with your stomach? Usually this is associated with anger, resentment, hatred, when you free yourself from that, "you heal."

Guilt directly affects the heart. I know perfectly well, at my *young age there came a time, when I thought my heart would no longer beat. The pain in my chest was constant, I forgave myself and let go of the guilt and all the symptoms went away immediately.*

When there is an absence of love, the skin dries out, withers, love is necessary in our lives, without love, even if I have everything in the world, I am nothing. God is Love, and everything that comes from love, nourishes, restores, edifies, prospers, fills, renews, revives, life takes on a magical and special meaning.

All types of addictions hide a type of void that we unconsciously want to fill, due to the absence of love, loneliness or sadness, we take refuge in them thinking that the false illusion of happiness will give us what we are looking for, but they only leave us in a worse state, with a feeling that makes us feel that we are worthless.

Problems with the lungs, it is a deep fear or great distrust towards living, breathing is life, and our breathing is what is affected by the lungs, an experience from the past, something that was done to us and it is very difficult to trust again and to want to live with the same joy as before.

Alzheimer's has its origin in the denial of reality, the pain is simply very strong, whether due to guilt or sadness from an event that marked us, such as the death of a loved one. Our mind tries to protect us from constant torture and decides to erase everything related from our minds; but little by little, it also takes away all kinds of memories, creating an imbalance in the brain that causes the disease.

The Light That I Carry in Me

Anemia arises from little interest in life, and in participating in it, being sleepy all the time, bored, which ends up affecting self-confidence.

Stones in the gallbladder, this is something that I suffered a lot, there were 5 attacks, and the pain is super intense, I felt like I was dying. Now I know that they were caused by bitterness caused by unexpressed hatred and resentment, I was holding to unnecessary emotions, I acted strong as a rock and never shared or expressed what was happening in my life.

Cancer is caused by multiple causes, taking into account the area where it develops, generally they are resentments or emotions that we have been carrying for too long, they are deep and painful wounds.

The intention of all knowledge is to correct our habits, to avoid future illnesses, everything we have in the present is the result of what we sowed in the past, and of the events and events that we suffer. By understanding how a disease originates, we can make informed decisions.

Consciously learn how to respond and manage all types of emotions, so that our health is not compromised.

If you suffer from an illness, and are currently being treated by a doctor, this is a complement that will greatly benefit your health. I firmly believe in natural preventive medicine, meaning eating healthy, exercising, sunbathing, drinking plenty of water, and above all, working on emotions and expressing them. Because what is outside does not harm the man, rather what comes out of the man, and comes out because it is what exists within, then being intoxicated with all kinds of emotions, the body has no defense and ends up getting sick.

Be aware of your body, it is your means of transportation to experience life on this earthly plane, and is the temple of God, we need to take good care of it.

There are many more information related to sickness and the relationship with emotions, a topic that I don't master jet, so if there is a sickness that you are experiencing or a love one, try to look for the information needed and how to help restore health by healing emotions!

The Light That I Carry in Me

CHAPTER 30

❦

It's In Our Hands

"Whatever we desire, believe that we have received it, and we will receive it"

Taking steps of faith, means taking action, moving towards what we want constantly, and with determination. There is only one time and it is now, it doesn't matter if we think about the past or the future, we can only live it in the now, so if what we want to receive it is something that we really want, we have to feel that it is ours now.
But how can I feel it from the now?
Using one of the most powerful tools we have, as spiritual beings in a world of matter: OUR IMAGINATION.
This is the key to safely manifesting all our desires. Tell me if it's not true that everything you see around you, was once a fragment in someone's imagination.

It is true and it is like this, everything begins with a question formulated in our head, or a thought that manages to disrupt our imagination, so that it begins. To work effortlessly in a number of possible scenarios, we just have to focus our attention, on the answer we are looking for, and we will obtain a solution that is sufficiently satisfactory. It all depends on an element that is fundamental for the process to be fulfilled, and have a greater impact, and this is: How badly do we desire what we are looking for?

Fireproof Knights

If the desire is so strong that it burns you inside, and does not leave you alone, then many solutions will come through your imagination; All you have to do is look for the one that best helps you achieve your purpose, with which you vibrate best, or with which you feel comfortable at this moment, then to take action, to execute the idea to check if it is what is appropriate. I often have a lot of ideas, which I consider can have a great impact on my life, I go to the next level, I simply write them down, as they come, no matter how absurd or not credible, my focus is on writing down, and over time return to the idea, modify it, add to it, subtract from it, wait to execute, or take action. If an idea comes to me, I consider that it has a purpose, maybe I don't understand it at the moment, but I know that sooner or later I will.

The problem is that we use our imagination to generate scenarios that generally go to a negative level. I remember when I was 9 years old, on one occasion my mother agreed to pick me up from school, I usually left around 1 o'clock. In the afternoon, but it was almost 3 o'clock, and there was no sign of her, so it was a good idea for me to return home alone. Since I didn't have the money to pay the fare, I explained to the bus driver what was happening to me, and he let me get on the bus, in the same way I did with the next driver. On the way back home, I was only thinking about my mother's joy when she saw that I could get home alone, but to my surprise I found her crying, she hugged me very tightly, she kissed me a lot and she couldn't stop crying, after a few minutes she stopped. She calmed down a little and told me: "I thought someone had kidnapped you, or that something had happened to you." She, then explained that she lost track of time to go pick me up from school, so the only thing she could do was imagine all kinds of scenarios where something could had happened to me! That combined with all the emotion, fear, anguish, desperation and guilt that she was feeling, created a

The Light That I Carry in Me

pair of moments when strangers approached me and were interested in me, in a different way, thank God the drivers were attentive to me and I arrived safely.

I don't blame my mother for anything, I am now a dad, and now I can understand her, but I also understand that it is up to us to remain calm and ask God with faith in the face of adversity, and then do what is in our power, keeping faith in God.

The moments that we have to have faith the most, it is when things are not as we expected to be, and push away all thoughts that steal our peace, because the imagination must be used to create, not to strip us of our tranquility, its purpose is to add not subtract.

We know what we want from life? We know what we don't want? When there are doubts it is because in reality the best thing is to wait, pay attention to our emotions, for them contain the power! They are like the gasoline that makes the engine run, whatever we really want, we have to feel it, and the stronger the desire, the easier it will be to obtain it.

How do you know if you want it and it's not just something you think you want? The easiest thing for me is to be close to what I think I want, and pay attention to how my body and energy react to it. For a long time, I thought I wanted a super luxury car, but when I had the opportunity to be close to one, I didn't even need to sit inside and feel all the comfort and elegance, just the thought of: "Where would I get in my children? There are many of us!", because for me the most important thing is to share with them, it's not that a luxury car is bad, it's just that at that moment it didn't vibrate with me. And this is how by exposing yourself to what you think you want; you confirm whether it is something that moves you to act or not. Whether it is something that makes you imagine an answer to be achieved, or not.

If you feel that it is something that you desire with a *fervent desire,* then move towards what you want because you will surely get it, and do not let doubt come between you and your desire.

For a moment imagine that you already have everything you want, the house of your dreams, the love of your life, the car you always wanted, the ideal business, how do you feel? What changed in you? How is your speech now? How is your attitude towards life? Now that you have a sample, why not make it permanent? Wouldn't you like to have it actually? If the answer is affirmative, would you change the way you dress? Would you change your way of seeing life? How would you treat the rest of people from now on? What could you do today to get closer to your purpose? What would you improve? You don't have to do much, just start! One brick at a time, and in a few years, you will have built a great wall.

The only thing you have to keep in mind is that everything has a time and space, there are things that have to wait, it is always good to prioritize what you want, and never get something at the expense of your happiness or that of someone else! It is It's better to take a little while, but I assure you that you will enjoy it even more.

The Light That I Carry in Me

CHAPTER 31

⚜

We are all One

"Like a drop of the sea, separated we are capable of nothing, united we are the ocean, we are all one."

We have to understand that the time has come when we have to think about the whole, take everyone into account, find a way to create a balance so that we can all be part of a better world, for a long time, we have sowed division and discord among us for unimportant reasons, and many times, that unimportant thing grew into a real problem.

Why don't we try from now on to create ties of brotherhood, without taking into account race or gender, I am from Guatemala and for a long time I was told that we are from the third world, like a select group of other countries, whether due to our geographical or sociopolitical position, but the truth is that there is no third or second world, there is only one and it is time to take care of it, it is time to change our mentality towards others, since we are healing, now we can see better, we can realize that we all need help, we are all going through something that we do not say for fear of being judged, mocked or not want to cause pity in others, let us have compassion for ourselves as a whole and instead of fostering division, let us begin to appreciate everyone, there are so many talents to share, so much knowledge, so much wisdom, we may not agree with everyone, but we can dialogue and find solutions that make us live in harmony and peace, we have to put love as a basis and appreciate each person, only by being more aware will we be able to heal a planet sick from so much evil.

It is incredible that we divide ourselves so easily, for whatever reason they make us enter into conflict, we are like rag dolls tied to imaginary ropes and moved at will. I listen to diverse opinions regarding what a man or a woman should be like, and it is in those opinions that division is fostered, it is so easy to recognize that we are all equal, what we carry inside is a soul that is limited by our body, what we are is much more than what our eyes can appreciate, the idea of adopting a role in this scenario is to interpret the best possible version, not to stay trapped in the character and defend to the death what we think is right, we focus on the least important and ignore the purpose that brought us here.

Why don't we start seeing the good in others, and forget about their flaws!

Let's build a culture of kindness and compassion!

The Light That I Carry in Me

CHAPTER 32

⚜

Messengers

God is speaking to us all the time, constantly and through all kinds of small signs, letting us know whether we need to keep going in the same direction or if we need to let go of the path we are walking! "We receive confirmations, reassurance or we get to feel a sense or inner peace or fear, self- doubt, anxiety" It is also very important to understand that the message can come from the least expected person!

Throughout history, we have received countless super important messengers, who have come to help us understand our purpose, they have come to show us how to live better, to explain to us what we truly are! They have come to reveal the way to live in harmony, but we have not believed them because of their humble origin, their traits, or for many other reasons. The truth is that it is easy to reject someone when we are blinded by our ego.

Generally, when something makes us react in a negative or even violently way, bringing out the worst in us, it is because we are facing someone who is making us see the truth, who is showing us something that we do not want to work with, or do not want to acknowledge! When we react to something, sometimes it means that there is us a problem, that needs to be worked on. Ask yourself the following question:

Fireproof Knights

Why do I react differently when I am in the presence of one person or another?
What is being revealed to me?
Why do these emotions control me and cause me to act differently than I want to?

The messengers come to tell the truth and that is what bothers, and like the evil that is in us, it has already settled and wants to continue inhabiting our being, it reacts and produces rejection, so the path to spiritual awakening is hard because we are continually exposed to everything, we do not want to see in us, that we must expel, change, heal, or understand in order to continue advancing in our spiritual processes.

Humility is not easy, it is what "the evil that resides in us" hates the most. Why do you think we pray kneeling? Because when we put ourselves in a position of service, it goes against the nature of the parasite; which is haughty, and it makes it uncomfortable and hides inside, and it is at that moment that we are ourselves, when our nature is revealed! And we realize that we are here, to serve one another!

Why do you think Master Jesus Christ often taught while washing the feet of his disciples? Have you ever done that for someone? I have had the opportunity to do it, and also to receive it, and on both occasions a connection free of ego was created, a space is created where we can see with spiritual eyes and recognize our nature, we create a communion between the participants where the doors to learning and teaching are opened.

The message is word, the word is life, not only by bread does man live but by every word that comes from the mouth of God. God is Love, every word based on Love comes from God, Love is a

The Light That I Carry in Me

spring of living water, water is life, the word of the true messenger quenches thirst, creates life, renews, and opens the doors to Love, for the same reason it creates conflict between father and son, husband and wife, between one person and another, but not because that is their intention, it is because "the evil that resides in one" reacts and wants to prevent the healing of the soul, wants to prevent the awakening of consciousness, creating a mirage where it makes us believe that tribulation is part of serving God, when it is only a sign of the detoxification we are going through. It is normal to enter a state of conflict at first, which will last as long as necessary according to the person, that is why we are urged to persevere and not give up. It is worth the effort, "definitely", I had never felt so much peace, love, happiness in my life just by opening my eyes in the morning, absolutely nothing else is needed to be happy, just to have the breath of life.

Focus on the message that the messenger of God carries! I'm not going to tell you, to stop going where you find God, I just ask you to set your eyes on seeking Him and the Holy Spirit, and pay attention to what you are taught. The intention of gathering is to learn from each other, not to indoctrinate, the intention is to learn to improve our lives, not to improve the lives of those who are in charge, the intention is to offer from our heart, but being responsible and aware of the proper use of funds, so that what we offer is a blessing for many, it is not intended that we be deprived of what we barely have, how can we give more and be more, if we do not have. Even consider a limit, a percentage, if you want to give more learn to generate more, but do not sacrifice what little you have, because God does not want sacrifices, what God wants is for you to be happy and to give according to the abundance you are creating and from the abundance of your heart.

Fireproof Knights

Be conscious of the beautiful and eloquent words that can turn out to be deceitful, the word must be with a sharp edge of a sword that penetrates within you and makes you feel it's true meaning, just be careful of those who entertain you thinking that the word of God is made for that, they have forgotten their purpose, that's all.

Do not judge them because they have served a lot, just that they have strayed from the path, remember that it is easy sometimes, to fall into temptation and make mistakes, but even being wrong in their tongues, they speak words of truth, just be careful that they are not intertwined with lies, so that you do not get confused, ask God for discernment and look at their actions, learn from the good, ignore what is not, do not focus on their faults, rather recognize their achievements and contributions, look at their fruits and recognize if it is wise to be part of that path, remember that most of the time we lead our entire families to believe in a truth that is not; we have to be responsible for ourselves and for them, just do not rush and ask yourself, am I really in the right place?

Just remember to have compassion for all who are in the service of God, the more you help, the more you are attacked, it is a path that is not easy but necessary, spiritual leaders are needed to help awaken their brothers through conversations, to foster learning, good values, forgiveness, and service directed towards those who need it the most, to be participants in a place where we support each other to grow and seek solutions for our society and the world we live in.

The Light That I Carry in Me

Messages have many interpretations; we need to take a prudent time to understand the meaning well. Messengers can be anyone and can come from anywhere, learn to see with spiritual eyes, search with determination and effort and eventually the truth will be manifested on to you.

For everyone who ask receives; he who seeks finds!

Fireproof Knights
NOTES

The Light That I Carry in Me
CHAPTER 33

⚜

The Wounds We Carry Within

A decision was made, a question posed, the answer to which would change everything. My mother, in the hospital with a pregnancy of 7 months, still nearly unconscious, needed to undergo a cesarean section. The chances of saving both were almost nil; a choice had to be made, and I was not the chosen one. By a miracle, by luck, or because there was a purpose, I clung to life. It was many months in an incubator, hoping to continue living; that is the story I know. I understand it's not easy for many families going through similar situations, but even if we don't understand, "I know God is with us, from the beginning, and He knows what's best for our lives."

From the moment we are in our mother's womb, we can perceive everything around us. We feel dad, we feel siblings, we feel other family members who are part of that space. We feel the vibration of the home, the music, the conversations; we feel everything! We feel mom's emotions, her fears, insecurities, sadness, anxiety. We feel whether we are rejected or accepted, and our body begins to communicate in the only way it can at that moment; biologically reacting, creating diseases, or showing superficially on the skin allergies or Irritation can lead to more serious issues like asthma or cardiovascular problems. Upon birth, we move to a stage where we can feel accepted or rejected. We remain fragile to our environment. As our situation develops, small wounds can begin to form, which over the years may heal on their own as our situation improves, or they can become larger and deeper.

This causes us to now express them through our way of being, our way of socializing, our way of viewing life. We are still very fragile and susceptible to our environment, with the difference that we are now a little more aware and can remember events. We are at risk of mistreatment, violence, and worse things. If these become too severe, they are wounds that can mark us very strongly.

From the age of 7, our brain is already programmed in a basic way, from that age onwards, we need to unlearn in order to relearn. In our life and everything around us, we already have a somewhat more defined way of being, and we begin to wear masks that allow us to navigate better. "If dad doesn't like children who cry a lot, we act strong and suppress our feelings and emotions." "If we realize what others expect of us and start pretending to be someone, we are not to fit in."

We can also pretend to be something more to get what we want; we have strategies we use without knowing, to make life easier for us.

Like lying, we learn to blame others to avoid punishment; we learn to omit facts or words, we learn to be silent, to be afraid, to flee. We get used to mistreatment, violence, abuse. We find others' misfortune funny, and it becomes normal for us; we think that's how it is for everyone, or we think we're the only ones going through a specific situation. We believe we are bad and don't deserve something good, which makes us react and behave rebelliously to our situation.

The Light That I Carry in Me

During adolescence, we are even more confused by the changes in our bodies; we begin to listen to all kinds of information that confuses us even more. Our emotions become more present; we move from anger to sadness to joy. We have needs in our body, and we don't know how to satisfy them or what to do with them. Judgments about ourselves or others begin to be more present, masks become clearer, and we start to use more masks because now we are exposing ourselves to more situations that require us to be different to feel accepted. We realize that by lying, we can do it more convincingly, and as the mini adults that we are, more trust is placed in us, and if not, we feel offended and react with blackmail. We use all sorts of strategies to draw attention; at this age, we think we know everything and want to experience life. That's why we are easy prey for alcohol, drugs, pornography consumption, or for people who may take advantage of us. We don't like to be corrected, and we easily approach everyone who thinks like us, regardless of whether it is right or wrong; we just care about being not corrected. It's a very difficult age because we even have the ability to create a life, which if so, complicates our own even more.

We become adults, and now our personality is more defined. We are what we think we are. Now we have a belief system that was nourished by everything we learned, saw, heard, felt, by all the experiences that marked our life. The wounds have now faded, healed, or are very large and infected; which generates that we have a different behavior, reactive when we are in situations that touch the wound again.

We become damaged adults and we go through the world encountering all kinds of situations that put us in contact with what we need to heal. Teachers appear; who can act as executioners, allies, victims, masters or saviors that help us work on what we need to learn, heal, understand. We fail to understand the purpose and go through life causing harm to others or allowing others to harm us. We think life is unfair and that there is no purpose in living it. It is at this moment that we realize we need to make a change, that we need to find a solution and pay attention to the wound we carry, but to heal it will hurt, possibly being the only way to heal it; we will have to open it again with the intention to cleaning it, disinfecting it, and healing it.

At any stage throughout our life before becoming adults, it would have been so easy to correct, unlearn, and relearn if only we had been paid attention, if only we had the information, if only someone had taught us how life works! The illogical thing is that we look for this information only when we are already damaged. There is so much information about life, and would be amazing if people care enough about helping and understanding one another.

We can make a big difference in the world around us, and it is with our experiences when shared, that we can be aware on how to go thru life rather waiting until we are hurt, damage or broken. None of us like to feel criticized or attacked by others, much less by the people we love, that is why we close ourselves to any advice, even if it is for our own good. We have to care enough to find the way to share the light we carry in us, so others can have a better view of how life is.

The fear tactic to control is more than clear, that is why we are told about a hell to instill fear and thus scare us into doing things right, but wouldn't it be better to awaken our conscience and being awake, be able to awaken the conscience of others?
I don't know about you, but I'm tired of so much violence in the

The Light That I Carry in Me

world. It is said that trillions of dollars are managed worldwide, but there is no capacity to end poverty or famine. We cannot have a decent retirement for our elders, we cannot provide food and shelter for the homeless, we cannot have an action plan for when someone makes a mistake, they have to pay with jail, where they come out more damaged and marginalized, making their rehabilitation almost impossible. We have all the tools to improve the world, but we are increasingly thinking about being more and more divided, many looking for what suits to them without taking others into account. Maybe it's too late for many of us to change, but it's not too late for future generations to learn a better way to live, a more conscious, intelligent, wise, and compassionate way! A more human way of thinking with the focus on finding the root of what is wrong, to have it replace with:

The Way, The Truth, And the Life!
"There is no other way"

Yes, it is something complicated, something very difficult to achieve, and even thought to be a fantasy, but the same is said about everything until it is achieved. All we need is for it to be possible by having a possibility, the doors are opened to a thought that seeks solutions through imagination, and it will already be in us if we take action to make a difference in the lives of others, in itself by taking responsibility in ourselves and seeking healing for ourselves, we become part of the solution because our presence matters and generates a change in our environment, and the light we carry can expand like a wave of energy through the world and reach every place of it

Let's identify the symptoms we have, and we will realize that there is a wound, sometimes we may have layers that have served as armor to protect us, we need to strip ourselves of the armor and *be vulnerable, it's okay to cry, it's okay to feel, it's okay to show what we feel, it's okay to feel resistance and not want to heal, it's okay to think that we are fine and that we do not need to change, what you feel is okay, but it is also okay to recognize that we need help if we are already tired of the life we have led so far. Because nothing will change if we don't change! There is no rush, we set the pace. If we decide to heal our wounds, then we need to "Heal the Past"*

Let's open our hearts and ask for healing from our Heavenly Father, believing that it will be done and by faith it will be so, just remember that this is a new opportunity to do it in a deeper and more conscious way where we have to focus completely on what happened to us and express it, we need to cry, talk, scream, whatever we consider necessary to start healing, we can do it alone or ask someone to accompany us and be part of our process, it all depends on the emotion we need to work on.

Why don't we want to heal a wound?
Is it Because of pain?
How many times do we not want to touch a wound?

All the time! Because it hurts a lot. It needs to be cleaned, exposed, disinfected, and this must be done more than once until it heals. Sometimes we just want to leave the wound as is, hoping it will heal on its own. Often it won't heal unless we do something about it. Then again, **It's on Us to Heal!**

The Light That I Carry in Me

CHAPTER 34

⚜

The Needs of Our Being

Have you ever confused thirst with hunger? Or have you been thirsty and wanted to quench your thirst with something other than water? What about water? Water can quench your thirst, as you can verify because you only drink the amount your body needs and the thirst disappears.

How many beers can I drink? As many as I decide. Will the thirst be quenched? No, because the function of a beer is not to quench thirst, then, what is its function? This is a question we should ask ourselves more often, for example: Have you ever had energy drinks? Why do you need energy?
Why?
What causes that lack of energy? If you compare yourself to a cell phone battery, where do you think your energy is running out? Because humans are not designed to seek energy, that is something our bodies produce automatically. All we have to do is learn to ask ourselves the right questions and learn. What foods do I need to eat, to have energy? What is depleting my energy? What can I do, to regain my energy? Or what should I stop doing, to not waste my energy?

One of the greatest needs we have is for Love, that's why when we truly approach God, we realize we don't need anything else to be well. God fills our tank! Now the question is, why does it empty so quickly? Sometimes we give so much love and it is not returned, or we have such a need for love, that we consume it too quickly. What consumes it? Burdens that we are dragging along,

due to customs, vices, wounds that we don't want to heal. But going back to love, what is a person looking for when they have many partners?
Are they looking for love?
Why is it sought?
Could be due to its absence?
What if you have someone, and you don't satisfy that absence?

We don't have to get confused; love is not sex or companionship! Love is love, just as water is water; there is nothing that can replace it; we are all in a world of need, especially after the pandemic. There are many people who are afraid or even panic at being in the presence of someone showing flu symptoms. There were several years where we were indoctrinated to distance ourselves from others, now our unconscious becomes defensive in the presence of anyone.

How can we reeducate ourselves?
By showing our mind that there is nothing to fear; creating love, hugging our loved ones, being kinder to strangers, and always looking for the good in others.

An unfaithful person has received a lot of damage or a strong blow that marked them, possibly a wound of deception that was not properly healed and reappears time and time again until it is healed. It's as if life puts us in the same situation again and again until we face it and decide to work on it. Deception makes us stop trusting other people, makes you feel less, makes you compare yourself to the other person wanting to find an explanation, a why, makes you feel that life is unfair and that true love does not exist, it dims you and makes you become an insensitive person over time, it is something terrible both to deceive and to be deceived. An unfaithful person acts without thinking and lives

The Light That I Carry in Me

with constant guilt; it is hell, especially when the person you betray "does not deserve to be betrayed on," but at the end, the deceived one is oneself! Because we do not realize that; if we still have the need, after being with another person or others, it is because we are not getting what we are looking for, so it's better stay in solitude and give proper time to heal, and to find out, what it is that we need!

And so, we can understand how the needs are manifested, because in the end, they all have a logical root, a person who mistreats others was mistreated or is being mistreated and needs to be emptying their cup because it is too much what they carry, so much so that even feels relieved to be in conflict because it releases a little of the stress that accumulates due to the situation.

A person who lies harbors a deep fear of facing reality. They might dislike their current life situation, and thus alter reality to make it more palatable, often at the expense of others. They are unable to acknowledge their true circumstances, which leads to the sowing of doubt and the creation of scenarios far removed from reality. It's a difficult cycle to break, and it's worth nothing that what might start as 'harmless' white lies can escalate as situations evolve. There are numerous reasons why people lie, but truth-telling is always preferable; eventually, time reveals the truth, leaving the liar embarrassed or shocked by the consequences. `

All is a matter of understanding ourselves and what are the needs we are experiencing and focus our attention on attend does needs to live in a more loving and caring way, if we are fulfilling this needs it will be easier to enjoy a full life and to understand others too, because we have a better idea of what might be happening in their lives too.

Fireproof Knights

If you need a little help trying to identify what you need to work on, then ask this question:
What need is being sought to satisfy?

When we are thirsty, we look for water!
When we are hungry, we look for food!
When we feel lonely, we look for company!
When we are cold, we look for warmth!
When we have needs, we look for help!
When help doesn't come from anywhere and we are in great need, we look for God!

Many times, we don't really look for God, until the emptiness and the sadness is so deep and the need becomes intolerable! And it is in those moments that we can transcend our inner being, and have a communion with our heavenly Father, and change our lives, but sometimes we fall and we look back to what we had, because the path of God is not easy, and following the right path is challenging and unpopular! We can feel misunderstood, alone and feel we aren't ready to left the old behind; is in this moment when we have to persevere and put our faith and trust in God's plan for our life.

All life has a purpose and is our mission to find it, and yes, we can be afraid to follow the way of truth, because we feel that we need to be perfect, but that is not the case, all we need to have been a willingly heart, and the desire to be part of the solution.

What happen if we are not perfect and we make a mistake again?

The Light That I Carry in Me

God is not looking for perfection, and we are here to learn, sometimes the only way to learn is by making mistakes. We don't have to get discourage and keep looking for God's way! God will be always there for us!

If we go back, we have to stop punishing us and think: why?
Why do I have this need to come back to my old me?
Why do I have this anxiety to do the same?
Why am I addicted to the wrong behavior?

There is a need, we need to identify; I can understand by my actions that the need hasn't been met, and unconsciously, we seek for what we are thirsty for. We can easily confuse ourselves with what we are looking for and take something else instead, it's time to reflect and ask what are my needs? And why?

And again, if there is something to heal, forgive or let go, now is the moment!

(Here you can go back to the chapter: "Let's heal the Past" on page 154 or you can continue reading)

Fireproof Knights
NOTES

The Light That I Carry in Me

CHAPTER 35

⚜

Appreciation

There is so much to appreciate and to give thanks for, every single day!

Women, from a young age, fill a home with joy with their unique ways. With their sensitivity and compassion, their hearts make the world pause when they begin to speak their first words to mom or dad. They are full of energy that is contagious; with a smile, they can light up the world. God made them perfect. Thanks to women, a man finds the inspiration to create. It is for women that a man decides to be more than he can be. The world is beautiful because of women; they are the light and calm in the storm, a source of inspiration. A woman is so unique and different; her beauty is matched only by her immense heart. How can we not appreciate them, how can we not love them? They are intelligent, sensitive, humble, and strong. They were made out of love, to give love, to create love. It is impossible to imagine a world without their warmth. They transform everything and make it better; you give them a house, and they make it a home. It is impossible not to love a woman.

On the other hand, men, how can I not remember my grandfather, a great man, hardworking, responsible, disciplined. Men are capable of everything and risk everything, especially for love. From a very young age, we love to help, we love challenges, and when we focus, we have the capacity to be and achieve anything we set our minds to. We have so many qualities that we develop to take care of those we love. We have a strong and brave heart; we carry so much that we choose to remain silent about because we love in a different way. We think differently, leading us to make decisions for the benefit of everyone. I fall short in truly describing what a man and a woman mean. God loves us so much that he gave us the perfect helpmate in each other. If we focus our abilities for the benefit of both, we will realize that everything is easier, everything flows smoothly, everything has a reason to be, and it is a privilege to share these two great strengths.

And this is just an example of what I do appreciate, if we go deep! We always can find a great number of different things for what we feel appreciation, lets connect with this virtue every day, lets share this energy with others! The more we show appreciation towards people we care about the better our relationship will turn to be! The more we show appreciation for all we have, the more we enjoy life!

Doing this is a life style, and just this habit by itself has the power to change completely our life and the way we approach to any circumstance!

And if we start seeing things for what they are really worth we won't have the time to hate, or be mad about insignificant things that don't really matter.

The shade of God is one of those things that make me feel so grateful, sometimes life can be challenging, complex and hard, but knowing that God is my Shelter, and under His shadow I can find rest! makes me feel safe, He will protect me even from the things I can't see! I can imagine for so many people around the world, when working on the fields in those hot days of summer,

The Light That I Carry in Me

what a shadow means! It must be hard being there long hours, working really hard, under the sun and then having the opportunity to rest under the shadow of a tree! I think they can truly understand and appreciate what being under the shadow means!

I definitely appreciate having food around and accessible thanks to all the hard-working people of the fields!

I am so thankful for all the people working in the hospitals, and we don't take the time to thank them, until it is the time when we need them. I remember when I was at the hospital after a terrible night of pain for the stones, when I woke up from the anesthesia, I was so thankful, until that moment I understood how important is their job!

I think we forget to appreciate so many things because in these days this, all is easily available, we don't really know scarcity, we are blessed, and we don't see it.

It is time to take a moment and just feel appreciation for all!

Thank you for giving me the chance to have this conversation!

I do appreciate it!

Fireproof Knights
NOTES

The Light That I Carry in Me

CHAPTER 36

❦

Lights, Cameras, Action!

We have worked hard on this book, from identifying reasons to fight, confronting our fears, realizing that we are the only ones responsible for our lives, knowing that diseases are the way our body communicates with us, understanding that the battle is in our minds, recognizing that the ego is a great adversary, but knowing that God is on our side every step of the way. We know that we push blessings away by not being on the correct frequency, that there are countless tools for healing, that our happiness depends on us, that love can do everything and is the basis for everything we set out to do. And now, what?

Now it's time to learn to take ACTION.
Planning is necessary, but too much of it can paralyze us, and that's precisely what we must avoid at all costs. It's like in a competition where runners hear: "On your marks! Get set!" and again "Get set!" and they never hear "Go!" They know that the chances of winning are slim; only one can take first place, but that doesn't matter. What they want is the chance to be the winners, they can only have that chance by competing; there is no other way. Taking action is the only way.

Imagination without action is useless. We can imagine the best idea in the world, a million-dollar idea, but if we don't act on it, it will never see the light of day, and the chances of someone else coming up with a similar idea over time are very high. Later, we will be left with the thought that "That was my idea!"

Just start, forget about being perfect, just start as you are. Take the step you can take now. Many of the great companies started from the garage of an entrepreneur, all with the illusion and vision of what could be. And that's what should motivate us, to set our eyes on the possibility of a better tomorrow thanks to that small step we are taking today.

We will always make mistakes; there will be thousands of details that we will need to solve. The important thing is not to take anything personally, just trust the process, make corrections, make adjustments, and try again. Success is achieved through perseverance more than talent. You may have the best product in the world, but consistency and determination are required to make your mark. Don't give up, insist, just ask yourself:

How can I do it better?
And the answers will flow so you can be better.
Put yourself in the right place. Many times, we are not where we should be, and that's precisely what prevents us from taking a step towards action. If you surround yourself with the right people who inspire you, who make you feel that achieving your dreams is possible, the chances of achieving it sooner multiply. Much is said about the 5% versus the 95%, assuming that only those in the 5% achieve all their dreams. To me, this is wrong; not everyone wants the same dreams, and perhaps we are looking for different things, which sometimes makes us lean more towards one percentage or move away from it, but this is irrelevant. Don't compare yourself, be happy with what you have now, and take action to continue filling yourself with experiences; that motivate you to go for more.

The Light That I Carry in Me

Nothing is impossible; we just don't yet know how to make it possible. That's the beauty of life, discovering how to do things. Humans are incredible; we have been capable of so much, but like in the time of the Tower of Babel, we do not understand each other, even speaking the same language, we are increasingly confused about what we think we want. "But it won't always be like this."

Give more than what is expected of you, and someday you will receive more than what you do. There's a belief I disagree with that I often hear in many workplaces: "That's not my job." Personally, I feel it shouldn't be like this. It's as if we were on the same boat that starts sinking after receiving an impact on the side, and I just watch as those on that side do their best to repair the damage and prevent the boat from sinking. I see this attitude constantly in many workplaces; taking action sometimes also refers to collaborating, to giving more than what is asked of us, to recognizing that someone is doing their best to provide us with a source of employment. Let's take action in learning, in helping, in improving what's not ours. I assure you; you will soon receive a blessing. Remember: You are sowing! When it's time to reap the fruits of your effort, you won't believe all that will be for you!

Sometimes all we need is someone to support us in moments of doubt or fear. Surround yourself with the right people, try to go to seminars or conferences, and meet people who are on the same mission as you. Try to establish a friendship with someone with the intention to both inspire each other to be better! commit to giving the best of yourself. You know, even lions are attacked by hyenas when they are alone. Many times, the mission we have can be a great blessing, and that's why it's important to be surrounded by the right people. Create alliances, and you'll see

Fireproof Knights

how everything becomes easier. Seek the right help for everything you need to do, create bridges of opportunity, and you'll feel great about yourself.

Let me tell you a bit about myself, not to brag, but rather to show you the power of God and what He has done and is doing with my life. As a starting point, let me tell you that I was born in Guatemala, where I lived until I was 9 years old, and then continued my childhood in the neighboring country of El Salvador. In both countries, I left pieces of my heart among friends, family, and memories (which I treasure with great love) in search of a better future I came to United States in 2005.

As an immigrant, with fears, insecurities, and many complexes that I overcame and left behind to make my way and find an opportunity, which, thanks to God, led me to own a franchise in the United States. The name of my company is Christopher & Ethan, and I have one of the brands that is gaining much acceptance at Grand Central Market in Los Angeles, California. "José Chiquito" is the name of the restaurant, and although we are a small company, we have managed to be in this market for many years, even going through recessions and facing crises like the global pandemic. It has not been easy, but God has always been with me, with my family, and with all the people who are part of our company.

Many have asked me, "How did you become a business owner?" To the surprise of many, I started working as a cashier in 2007 with very little English. I managed to get an interview with the then-owner of the place, Steve. I remember he asked me many questions, most of which I answered with a simple "yes." I didn't have much knowledge of the language to answer better, but I needed to work, and I got the job. My mission from the

The Light That I Carry in Me

beginning was to prove to my boss that he had not made a mistake with me. I took it as my own from the beginning, worked many overtime hours, and never charged for them. I wanted to learn everything related to the business, worked 7 days a week, and focused on preparing myself for an opportunity. Over time, I learned English, learned all areas of the restaurant, became a manager, and without the possibility of buying a car, I had to make some emergency purchases on my bicycle. I assure you; I had no idea what I was doing, but I had the will to push the business forward. I improved and improved, and the results got better until the moment came when I could become the owner of the place. It has been 16 years of effort and dedication. I educated myself as best I could through books, business coaching seminars, personal coaches, spiritual guides, hours of training on the internet, audiobooks, study programs, and many mistakes that I paid dearly for but were necessary to get to where we are now. There have been hundreds of small changes, modifications, attempts, and retries. I have lost thousands of dollars that I now see as investments in my education. In one way or another, we have to pay the price if we want to achieve something in life. At the same time that I was building a company, I was losing my life, or it was the focus on the business that helped me stay afloat in the hardest years. That and, above all, God's help, which in one way or another always took care of me. He knew I needed it because now, looking back, I realize I was never alone. I can see God's hand in every moment, even in the time when I worked while depressed, when my heart failed me, when I had gallbladder attacks, when we didn't have enough to pay the rent for the business, much less the rent of the apartment, in all the times I wanted to give up on me, now I recognize that God helped me by putting me in charge of a business because, thanks to the restaurant, I was able to take my mind off the situation. What I want to say with this is that there will always be a thousand and one problems for not doing what you want to do, but it is precisely when you have to do it the most!

I clung with all my might, for myself and especially for my children; because during all this time, and upon analyzing myself, I realized that I had to become someone completely different from who I once was to understand that:

1. "If I change, everything changes."
2. "Daring to take that leap of faith is the best thing."
3. "It was 16 years of my life that would have passed anyway"
4. "The foundation always has to be love."
5. "The only person I deceived was myself."
6. "That we can all be better."
7. "It doesn't matter how; God will provide what you need."
8. "The path is made by walking."
9. "Problems are part of life."
10. "Knowledge is nothing if not put into practice."
11. "We all have the opportunity to achieve a life that resembles paradise here on earth."
12. "Great battles are won on our knees and in prayer."
13. "We can't do it alone; we depend on everyone."
14 "We are all at the service of someone else."
15. "Thank God for everything at all times."
16. "the personal achievements are even more important, if shared."
17. "Surround yourself with the right people."
18. "Avoid distractions."
19. "Honor all teachers, even if you don't agree; they deserve respect."
20. "Money is a tool; use it as such."
21. "Stay calm in the face of anything that takes away your peace; it's necessary."

The Light That I Carry in Me

22. "Enjoy life more."
23. "Love yourself as much as you can."
24. "Saying No, is a Yes for you."

The purpose of my story is just to show you that if I can do it, you can too! We set our own limits because if we focus on what we don't have or are not, nobody would do anything. You don't have to see the entire path or know what comes next, just move forward, walk, and as you do, the rest will clear up so you can see a little more, and that's how you'll achieve what you set out to do.

Do what you need to do every day; don't worry (don't preoccupy yourself) about tomorrow, do the best you can do today, and so every day.

Now is the time when we no longer make excuses and go for what we want, go for the life we've always dreamed of, become our best version. It doesn't matter if we still have a lot to heal, it doesn't matter if we still have doubts, it doesn't matter if fear dominates us at times, nothing else matters but being happy.

From now on, I assume the role that corresponds to me to become, who I must be. The camera is ready; everyone is waiting for the main actor to come on stage. That's me! I won't make them wait any longer and will give my best performance I know it won't be easy; there may even be times when I want to quit, but those moments will be brief because now I am in a different state of consciousness.

When I feel like I'm about to lose purpose, I'll pause, but I won't back down until the ticket to be here in this world is taken away from me, when the game is over. Until then, until that moment comes:

Fireproof Knights

I will give my best,
I will surround myself with people who inspire me to live a wonderful life,
And to be always part of the solution!

Until that last moment
　　I will continue to share

　　The light that I carry in me!

The Light That I Carry in Me

CHAPTER 37

⚜

Let Me Tell You a Story

Marlon, *I share the following story with you, hoping you will open your heart and just listen without prejudice, without believing, without disbelieving, just feel the truth, that's all; if something in you resonates, perfect; if not, perfect.* **One of my spiritual teachers told me**:

"This is something that resonated with me!" Take it as you see fit"

Today I share this story with you:

It turns out that the earth is nothing more than a place where you can experience, where you have the opportunity to learn, where you come to create consciousness and evolve to a higher plane.

Through reincarnation, you have come multiple times with the sole intention of learning. And with a very specific purpose: to HELP. That's why, no matter what you think of yourself, when you help, something inside you lights up, and this happens because that's your purpose from the beginning.

We all share a spiritual plane before coming to this world; many of us know each other, many others have strong ties and bonds because we have shared more than once some role in the game of life. You have been a father, mother, son, daughter, husband, wife, you have been the victim, you have been the victimizer, you have *been born in different countries, circumstances, in different times, you have learned, and you have forgotten. Your DNA holds everything well-guarded. And all our history is stored in the Akashic Records. It is then that from this beautiful spiritual plane, we decide to come here to earth to learn, to help, to be better because every time we come, humanity as a whole seeks to reach a higher level of consciousness.*

We all have to cross the threshold between the spiritual and the earthly plane. And that's when we need a means of transportation between the two. Our parents are chosen by us for multiple reasons and also because they are the right ones for the lesson we come to learn, for the wounds we come to heal from past lives, or to heal the generational wounds of our ancestors and predecessors, to be specific, 7 generations before and 7 generations after.

Many children, even before the age of 5, can see the spiritual world, remember who they were in another life. It is the case of one of my sons; he mentioned that in another life he was older and had died in a fire, and curiously, he showed a mark on his body and said, "Look, this is a mark from that moment."

Many of us already knew each other before coming and have the opportunity to come through the same parents, in which case the siblings are very close. In other cases, the siblings did not know each other, and as they grow up, they have an endless number of differences that prevent them from being close. Many times, the same siblings or parents begin to show us what we must heal, playing a role that activates that wound, and over the years, we encounter situations and people who, in one way or another, touch the same point again. And this wound is something we all experience, but we go through life believing we are the only ones.

The Light That I Carry in Me

And definitely, we all come to this place to work on something or to heal something.

The important thing is to recognize as soon as possible what kind of wound you have and study how to heal it. There are a number of teachers who can help you heal; it is up to you to understand the problem, seek healing.

Then life becomes our school, and it is also like a video game where your mission is to learn, improve, heal, help other participants to understand the purpose of all this; but above all, the greatest purpose of all is to experience, because as a spirit, we cannot, "everything is theory" here on earth is where you practice. And when your time is up, you simply wake up again in the spiritual world. With many familiar faces waiting for your return to our true home.

This is the version that resonates with me, the one I choose to believe. Again, I tell you, what you decide to believe is personal. Don't believe me, prove everything, feel it, and decide for yourself.

Fireproof Knights
NOTES

The Light That I Carry in Me

CHAPTER 38

⚜

Collectors

After giving it, some thought and with the heart, we can conclude that if we are here in this world, it is to acquire knowledge and tools to live better experiences and to have a good time. It's that simple, but as it's simple, we tend to complicate it more. We have the habit of complicating things in our minds because we need a super logical explanation taken from a quantum physics book to believe it's true. And then we expect to do little to get a lot out of life.

The answers are simple; the hard part is doing, going for what we want, and staying constant day after day. That's why it gets complicated for everyone because the path is full of obstacles and difficulties, but that's exactly what makes it so rewarding when we achieve a goal.

A new way of seeing things for me has been to become a collector of experiences, not things or wealth, but of experiences that make me feel alive and that, over time, I can remember and relive through those memories, living each day with the illusion that even in the most ordinary and normal of our daily routine, we take a moment to deliberately create magic and special moments. Imagine you are the main artist in your movie, and the cameras are focused on what you are doing; everyone is watching, everyone is on pause waiting for what will happen next. It is at that moment that you have to feel and do something that makes everyone vibrate with emotion; you can sing with your soul, laugh until you feel like you might wet yourself, play your favorite sport as if it were the final of a soccer World Cup, give the best of you, don't hold back: sing, laugh, vibrate with emotion, fall in love, love, inspire, speak with your soul, express your feelings, put on your favorite music and dance as if it were the last time you would do it. In everything you do, act as if you were trying to win an Oscar. I assure you; your life will never be the same. It will change the meaning of everything, and you will make your days and those around you memorable, impacted by your joy and enthusiasm, wanting to be like you.

How beautiful it would be to live like this every day of your life, giving your 100% even in the most mundane, making life not guaranteed at all and at any moment, our ticket to enjoy. Because that is the intention, to enjoy, to take from this world the greatest number of memories to enjoy later. Do you have a movie that you love to watch, one of those that you never get tired of and could watch many times? Do you have a song that you love, that moves you, that makes you dance and sing? Is there a sport that you love, that makes you vibrate with passion? Do you have people in your life that you will surely miss?

Remember to let them know every day that you love them, let them feel your presence wherever you go, bring rays of light and faith, make every moment worthy of being remembered, and get used to going to bed satisfied every night for having done something that improves your life.

This is your life; create a masterpiece out of it. You are the main actor. Never forget it; dare to shine because that's why you came to this world. You are important, and you make a difference, and

The Light That I Carry in Me

with your life and work, you will leave a legacy that will last for generations.

Let's Gather memories to cherish!

Fireproof Knights
NOTES

The Light That I Carry in Me
CHAPTER 39

⚜

Hell

This topic is as easy to understand as it is complicated. It all depends on our level of consciousness and having a mindset free of prejudice and beliefs. It's not a topic for debate or wanting to be right, just to analyze and be open to the possibility, of a reality different from; what we've been taught through history.

Hell does exist, but it's because we create it by believing in it, it becomes a place that houses many souls together because they also believed in it. Its purpose is punishment and suffering, torment, and pain at unimaginable levels. When I tell you we are children of God, I am telling you my truth, and from there, I easily understand that we all have a creative power within us. We can create hell here on earth; on a material plane, and it will be even easier to create hell on a spiritual plane, what the person has decided they deserve after their life ends based on how they lived. It is the same consciousness that makes us feel shame, and guilty for our actions, and by feeling that way, we are convinced that we deserve some kind of punishment for our believe system.

For so many when we were little kids, we were told to behave in certain way, whether with scolding, yelling, harsh words, beatings, or punishments. So many of us were programmed to receive a punishment for every time we didn't do good and depending on the mistake or sin, so the size of the punishment! anyone can stumble on a path, especially when trying to learn. I don't know anyone who, when faced with several math operations, doesn't fail in the answer on more than one occasion, and I don't see anyone saying you're going to hell for that.

Yes, there are errors that are too strong and fatal, but all because we are programmed through video games, movies, newspapers, magazines, conversations, and that's why we accept violence as something normal. We are shocked and outraged when we live through a situation of violence close to us, but it is practically indifferent to us when other unrelated people live it. We become insensitive to the pain and suffering of others; we become judges easily and dedicate ourselves to promoting gossip without knowing all the details.

We condemn and wish harm according to how the facts were explained to us, but we are not interested in knowing what causes a person to reach such an extreme decision in which they reacted against their nature. We need to know their story, to understand how to prevent it from happening in another person again; and on top of having to paid so much here in life, an eternity in hell, waits for them. I don't know about you, but I DON'T BELIEVE IN A PUNISHING GOD! It seems illogical to me; life is an instant compared to eternity, and for a mistake in that instant, we are going to live an eternity of torment. **I know is not light that!**

God is love, life, intelligence, and the idea of hell is based on fear, death, and stupidity, which seems to be the complete opposite of what God is to me; Therefore, I think the cunning of evil sowed its tares in the very book that was intended as a manual for a beautiful life of learning and experimentation, with the purpose of instilling fear and all kinds of sensations that keep

The Light That I Carry in Me

us away from our goal, "To Enjoy a beautiful experience on earth."

The hell I experienced.
I had the opportunity to deeply understand what my being believes would be hell for me, and my experience led me to be part of the matrix, as if inside a video game, where my vision suddenly had the ability to perceive reality in pixels and codes, modifying the perception of everything known as matter, and giving it a more real name, "energy."

I found myself being part of a gear, as if the entire world were a hologram, and by placing my face on the ground, I could see what was inside: a machine creating the reality we know. I saw how my face joined this machine and felt the helplessness, the cold, the suffering of my soul for being just another part of the gear. A piece of matter without life, without power, without meaning, without control.

It was something terrible; I remained practically in this hell for a time that escaped my perception. I didn't know if it was hours, minutes, or seconds that had passed. But being in a state of full consciousness, I defeated it by simply letting go of fear, letting go of the illusion's deceit, and realizing that everything was a dream, that the nightmare only has power if you allow it, that you yourself are responsible for what you are going to experience, that the ego and the evil within us; use all kinds of tricks to convince us that we deserve hell. But even in a deep darkness and completely paralyzed by fear, there is a voice that comes from within, loud and encouraging us to not give up, a voice that reminded me that everything is fine! that I always been! and I always will be! an exact and powerful mantra that restored strength and confidence in me, and I knew that God is always with us at every moment, but we often don't feel it because we *don't pay attention to our interior, the outside noise is too loud.*

Upon analyzing my experience, I have been able to understand, that precisely for me, hell would be a place where I had no freedom, where I had no choice whatsoever over my being. For everyone, it will be something completely different. I don't know what hell you are going through or think you are going to go through, but even being in that place of death, redemption, and life can be found if only we believed and sincerely repented, even there is forgiveness!

We can defeat the beast spoken of in the apocalypse because the beast is us when our senses are dominated by ego; we are the creators of wars, genocides, immoralities, perversions, evil beyond a horror story. Dominate the beast and win by raising your consciousness.

It's never too late for a change, never too late for a new beginning, never too late to be better, never too late to avoid hell.

The Light That I Carry in Me

Fireproof Knights
NOTES

The Light That I Carry in Me

CHAPTER 40

⚜

The Traps of The Ego

There comes a time when we feel healed and leave things half-done. We must stay firm for longer and, above all, stay alert because we have let go and removed so much garbage that we were carrying without any sense. "Remember, the enemy prowls around like a hungry lion, just waiting for the slightest moment to attack," especially when we haven't filled that space with positive habits and feelings that keep us at a higher vibration level. We run the risk of returning to old habits that had us imprisoned, risking becoming victims again, and even falling lower than we ever were.

The ego is the one that, when we are well, makes us forget about God, our loved ones, our friends. It makes us forget all these people who were there by our side, who helped us and gave their best for us to achieve our goal.

The ego is that voice that tells us we don't owe anyone anything, that we got out of where we were "all by ourselves." But if we take a moment and truly remember, we will realize that there were countless times when, in anguish and desperation, we cried out for help! Sometimes we didn't even know what to do with our life. There were moments of fear and panic when we didn't see the way, moments when many people helped us get to where we are

Fireproof Knights

now. But now we say: it was all thanks to me and my effort alone! now that we are in a better life situation, economically speaking, now that luck has smiled on us, and we have let go of all those limitations from our past. I have news for you: this new level brings other traps, more subtle to identify, such as: indifference, idolatry, gluttony, love for money and power, despising others for what they are going through, for what they have achieved, or because they are lost and full of bad habits that keep them tied down in misery on the brink of death, so know we call other people nicknames like cheap, looser, brock, lazy, nobody, mediocre, etc.

It is at this moment that I ask of us: now that we are in a better situation, let us not forget where God took us from. We come from being slaves in Egypt, we have crossed the desert, and now that we are well, that we are on our way to the promised land, the ego becomes present and tells us to look back with what we have now, and said that we did it alone!

No way! *"Without God we can't do anything"*

Many will make others believe they are gods, now that they have power, be careful because many will seek to take advantage of the illusions of many by selling them a dream, telling them that they have the recipe for happiness, showing themselves as winners, squandering money and flaunting everything they have and the life they live! to seduce as many blind people as they can. Be careful of the false prophets that are leading many to ruin. Remember, the god they serve will discard them when no longer pleased with their results.

In the spiritual, it attacks us in a different way, where it asks for recognition for every person we help, whether with knowledge,

The Light That I Carry in Me

tools, or any kind of help we provide for our neighbor. Everything comes from God, and when He provides the talents, the tools, and everything necessary for us to be a blessing, we have to give honor to God, and we will receive a reward without even asking for it or needing it, because when we serve the absolute truth, we are in a privileged place. God will comfort our soul, our cup will overflow, and in God's presence, we will find everything we could have ever dreamed of.

Do not let the ego steal your blessing, do not let it deceive you, do not let its cunning make you think it is intelligent. There is only one "Infinite Intelligence," and the ego has no part in it.

Be strong and steadfast, forge a character that is difficult to bend, and every day, get on your knees not because God needs worship. Everyone has been confused with this; when you get on your knees, your ego "can't stand it" and goes away, hides, and when it's far away, that's when you can truly commune with God, really feel him, and he can show you, his love. He will bring comfort to your soul, joy to your heart, and you don't have to be on your knees all the time because when God is present, everything that is foreign to his essence has to go. But remember, it is free will. God will never impose anything on you, much less himself so that you seek him. If it is in you to approach God, do it; if you don't feel it, it's okay. Nothing happens. I assure you he will always be there. He is eternal, remember?

And HÉ loves you; you are His "creation."
Never forget this!

Fireproof Knights
NOTES

The Light That I Carry in Me

CHAPTER 41

❦

Waiting For Gods Timing?

We are told that we have to wait for God's timing, but is the word "wait" the correct one? I believe it's about doing our part and taking action, seeking what we want, what makes us happy, what corresponds to us as children of God. But by doing so, are we showing a lack of faith?

Or are we misunderstanding the phrase WAIT FOR GOD'S TIMING? We often take words lightly, saying them just for the sake of saying them, and giving them a meaning that is often completely removed, from their original purpose. We need to start analyzing the language we use more carefully, to truly understand the instructions, on what we should do and to really understand the hidden message; that each word holds. We may think this is very difficult and that it would take a lot of time, but I believe it's better to make the effort to learn because otherwise, we could spend years walking in the opposite direction of what we want just because we didn't understand from the beginning, that we were walking in the wrong direction!

This is something that has been very difficult for me to understand. I lived in a hurry for a long time thanks to a book I read when I was about 19 years old, which said that one of the great secrets of successful men was "walking fast."
There was a sense of urgency in them; it seemed that wherever they went, they had to arrive quickly and leave with the same speed, and my way of thinking from that moment was modified,

Fireproof Knights

and I began to do everything faster with the belief that this would make me a successful man. The advice has taken me far, but by living in a hurry, thinking about getting to my destination quickly, I have lost, on many occasions, the sense of the journey. Seeking to give more meaning to my life and with the idea of being a successful man in any project I decide to undertake, I have adapted to various life philosophies where I have understood that "It's not about arriving quickly, what's important is how we arrive."

Now I think more about enjoying the journey in life, giving myself the opportunity to take the time to reach my destination in a more conscious way, with health and happiness from the decisions I have made, and above all, in peace. But I have realized that I have always wanted to have control over my life, and just the idea of not having it scared me a lot, which is why I learned to wait on God and understand that the purposes I give to my life are the right ones. The time we have is short, so it is wise not to prolong things that are unnecessary, not to prolong suffering, pain, adversities. Let go soon and focus on what we want will always be the best.

Waiting for God's timing literally, the word "wait" means "to stay in one place until a person arrives or something happens," and it comes from Latin sperare: "to have hope," and having hope means "to trust in achieving something or that something desired happens." we live in matter, so we are governed by its laws, God's timing is when it is the right moment, it is always perfect, it is we who delay in learning the lesson; that corresponds, and prolong more than necessary, what should be, we carry more than necessary, by decision, we cling and make ours any problem or adversity. We say my problem, my illness, my misfortune, we make ours- things that don't belong to us! we wait on God for a

The Light That I Carry in Me

solution, we pray and pray for healing, for happiness, for love, for peace, for money. Let's not just wait for problems to solve themselves, let's put our faith in God, let him do His part, what corresponds to Him, and let's think about what corresponds to us and act accordingly. Many times I have been going through situations that are too big for me, and I do not find the solution, and I feel anguish, and I feel angry, and I feel sad, I know that I cannot go to my father's house, that is when; I closed my eyes and pray, so I ask for forgiveness for my attitude and then I ask for a solution with the certainty that it will be resolved soon, I feel that everything is fine, I deposit my faith in God and let go of the problem, I give thanks and continue my day with a positive attitude, I try to smile a lot, showing faith in my actions, in my voice, and in my face because I know that God will provide and the solution will manifest itself. In a short time, out of nowhere, an idea comes to me that, by taking action based on it, brings the solution, and it is at that moment that I realize that God has control of my life and everything, and I was practically drowning in a glass of water. There is a solution for everything, always, and it comes with wisdom, which cannot be obtained without going through difficulties. Sometimes God's timing makes us test our faith because it is very easy to succumb to adversity, especially if we feel we are alone. However, we must remember that we have never been alone, we are surrounded by God's love, and that love is eternal, unique, and true, and because we are all children of the same Father, we are not alone, we choose to be alone, but there are hundreds of brothers around us with whom we could share a moment of true light.

Fireproof Knights
NOTES

The Light That I Carry in Me

CHAPTER 42

❦

Who is God?

The truth about this is as simple as it is complex because, I don't believe in God, I know God, for me He is a loving Father. I did not have the joy of having a father; I always wished for one, and when I had the opportunity to be in God's presence, He felt my void and absence and granted me that gift, that which I always wanted! God became my Father; He advises me, cares for me, guides me, lets me make mistakes, lets me learn from them, allows me to grow and mature at my own pace, has patience with me, shows me the path to take, helps me gain wisdom through lessons and learning, helps me understand my purpose here on earth, helps me understand everyone's purpose here on earth, blesses me and prospers me, I understand completely that I am the one responsible for my actions, so I am the one being bless or pushing His blessing away!

He is always attentive to me and my needs and concerns, keeps away from me things that harm me, heals and restores me continuously, and above all, gives me His love and teaches me to truly love myself and to love my brothers in the right way. For you, God may be a loving Mother, a brother, a Prophet, a teacher.

We cannot limit God; He is everything, He is the universe and all its extension and more. He is continuous, present, and omnipresent, was, is, and will be. He is everything and is in everything that exist and in each one of us.

Fireproof Knights

He has qualities that make Him unique:

Truth. It is eternal and constant, silent, powerful, it does not need to impose itself, it just is.

Love. It is eternal, permanent, constant, always is and will be.

Intelligence. Intelligence is eternal and is everywhere forever and ever, in an atom, in a plant, wherever you see, there is intelligence.

Life. Because it always is, there is no death, only transmutation.

Unity. We are part of God like droplets of water in the sea, united to Him but at the same time individual, and likewise in everything that exists.

beginning. There was a beginning for everything! and there is always a beginning! And the end is always the door for a new beginning!

God is eternal and true, removed from material laws, He is incapable of dying, aging, being corroded, degraded, or hurt, He is everywhere at the same time, He is consciousness, God is everything.

For a long time, I was very angry with God because I blamed Him for everything bad that had happened to me and for the bad in the world. Why doesn't God do anything about it? Why does He allow evil? Evil and badness are in us; He loves us and can only wait for us to learn to prevent evil from controlling our lives and our decisions.

I have had the opportunity to be a father, and one of the most difficult moments I faced was when I found out that one of my

The Light That I Carry in Me

children was diagnosed with autism. All kinds of terrible thoughts came about the condition of my son, but above all, many complaints to God. Even going so far as to say, "Why me, when there are plenty of parents who deserve to have a child like that?" "Why me if I am good?" I didn't know what I was saying! Christian is one of the greatest blessings I have received; he is an angel, and his way of loving is unique. It is a privilege for me to have him in my life. Yes, the challenges are different compared to some of my other children, but his purpose is great, and what he brings to my life is wonderful. Thank God for him!

It is not until we recognize that God is not to blame for anything, He has given us life and overall: free will! Along with many other tools to be creators of our environment, it is up to us to do a good job.

The detail is that we filter what God is with a mind that, although unique and privileged, is very limited and cannot comprehend what God is. Even the word God limits Him, my intellect and wisdom cannot find anything similar to describe such a supreme being, I fall short, and so far, there is no way to describe it, and to understand everything that it represents.
Perhaps one day we will be able to comprehend all that God truly is, what I know for sure is that God; is the creator of all that is and exist!

And I know He is there for us, at every step of our life, what we have to understand is that we have to intentionally focus on God in everything we do, and who can be our true master to help us become apprentices? Yeshua "The Lord is Salvation"

Is clear why we need "Salvation" because there are many who doesn't have Love in their hearts for instance all the bad in the

Fireproof Knights

world today.

Someone may asked why exist the bad in the world! Isn't God the creator of everything?

To experiment life on earth has to be a duality!
The cold doesn't exist but is produce by the absence of the hot
The darkness doesn't exist but is produce by the absence of Light
And evil exist in people because there is absence of God in us!

We are the place where God lives! But we can't feel his presence because we don't take care of the temple! We are choosing to live without Him in our lives, ang go thru life experimenting all! And we can choose to go after all material things, but at the end is a mirage of happiness, there is not real glory in the material world, that's why we have to focus on looking for God and his glory first and all will be added to us, "all that we really need!"

With God we might not have everything that we may desire, because at the end He knows what is best for us! So, we have to take a step back and understand why sometimes we don't receive all we ask for!

I hope we can see him thru the innocence of a child eyes, and understand that is time to retake the core values that as a women and men of God should have! I think we have to realize after so many years of trying our way without God, where that is leading us?

And with all this I am not trying to convince you of anything! Or to make you believe in God!
But to go deep in your heart, and ask what's real? and give

The Light That I Carry in Me

yourself an opportunity to feel and ask what if?
What if is real? And I am not giving me the opportunity to have a relationship with Him!

What if I am missing out of the most beautiful love than can exist?

What if that's what I have been looking for?

What if God is the real path thru real happiness?

What if God is nothing like I have been told?

What if God only wants to have a close, real and meaningful relationship with me?

What if I discover in His presence that He is all that I ever needed?

Is it too hard to give ourselves the opportunity to try His way?

Is it really, that bad to give it a try?

I am giving me the opportunity! And deep inside I know I am making the best desittion ever, I love been in his presence! **I know God!** and I personally, will continue to call Him Father!

I know who can help me get even closer to Him, and who can lead us to His ways, **our master Jesus Christ!**

Fireproof Knights
NOTES

The Light That I Carry in Me
Last Words

From the bottom of my heart, I thank you for reaching to the end of the book, I hope you have founded the answers, the tools, the knowledge and above all the opportunity to know God thru my eyes!

My intention is not to convince you of anything, but to wake up in you, the desire to learn, to find the answers, and to believe again in a new opportunity! I know if all of us raise the level of consciousness, we will be able to align our life; with a new vibration, that will help us live, the life we deserve!

May your mission in life be to find The Way, The Truth and The Life!
I am another student, I need still a lot to learn, and I really hope to be of service for so many years, I will continue to keep on learning so, I can share with you more wisdom and knowledge.

God bless us and He may fill our hearts with so much love, so we can share his blessings with many more, and we may touch the hearts of those who still sleep and have the opportunity to awaken them!

Fireproof Knights

It is my time to say good bye, but I want to do it with two questions for the next time we meet again!

*Now that I have more knowledge and tools:
will I keep them hiding?
Or
I will share The Light That I Carry in Me! to become the Fireproof Knight that exist in me?*

The Light That I Carry in Me

Fireproof Knights
NOTES

The Light That I Carry in Me

About The Author

⚜

The message will be always more important than the messenger, I just hope to have touch your heart, I am just someone who believes in God and is trying to make a difference in the life of somebody else!

If you can help me, share this book and if possible, leave a review on amazon to reach more people that would be amazing!

With deep appreciation and gratitude

Marlon Medina

Son of God

Fireproof Knights

The Light That I Carry in Me

Table of Contents

It was no longer me 7
The number 7 13
What if what you think it is, isn't what it seems? 15
An Encounter with My Creator 18
Everything has a beginning 23
Few Are the Chosen 24
Truth is a Sphere 27
Ferrari 30
Take Responsibility of Yourself 33
Take Action 37
About us? 41
With Our Thoughts, We Change Our World! 45
Don't Use God's Name in Vain 49
Ask in a Good Way 52
Everything has a frequency 57
Express What You Feel 61
The True Teachers 65
Pay the Price 69
What Do You Want from Life? 73
The Base Is Love 77
Forgiveness is The Way 85
JUST FORGIVE! 86
It's time to free ourselves! 87
Don't Compare Yourself 91

Fireproof Knights

Let go and trust 95
Look for the good in everything 103
The Truth About Money.. 107
Give Thanks for Everything, At Every Moment!............................ 113
My love 117
It's Okay to Say "No"... 123
The Power of Words 129
Only One Time Exists 133
Attitude... 137
A Three Part Story 141
Second Part 144
Third Part 145
"You are the pearl that I took from the sea" 145
With The Fear in Hand.. 149
Our True Nature 159
Let's Heal the Past... 163
Pray Without Ceasing 169
Always Healthy 173
It's In Our Hands... 177
We are all One.. 181
Messengers 183
The Wounds We Carry Within.. 189
The Needs of Our Being 195
Appreciation... 201
Lights, Cameras, Action!... 205

The Light That I Carry in Me

Let Me Tell You a Story **213**
Collectors **217**
Hell **221**
The Traps of The Ego **227**
Waiting For Gods Timing? **231**
Who is God? **235**

Fireproof Knights

7

Fireproof Knights

Made in the USA
Columbia, SC
31 August 2024